OM

the eternal witness

OM
the eternal witness

SECRETS OF THE MANDUKYA UPANISHAD

Swami Rama

Himalayan Institute Hospital Trust
Swami Ram Nagar, P.O. Doiwala
Distt. Dehradun 248140 Uttarakhand, India

Editor: Prakash Keshaviah, Ph.D.
Cover design by Connie Gage

Reprint 2020

Library of Congress Control Number: 2007927732
ISBN 978-81-88157-43-3

Published by:
Himalayan Institute Hospital Trust
Swami Ram Nagar, P.O. Doiwala
Distt. Dehradun 248140
Uttarakhand, India
tel: 91-135-241-2068, fax: 91-135-247-1122
src@hihtindia.org, www.hihtindia.org

Distributed by:
Lotus Press
PO Box 325
Twin Lakes, WI 53181 USA
www.lotuspress.com
800-824-6396

Contents

Foreword

In the very first paragraph of this book, H.H. Swami Rama declares, "This knowledge which I am giving you has not come through my mind. . . . This knowledge comes through inner vision (revelation)." Later he tells us that he studied the Mandukya Upanishad 22 times but did not understand it. Understanding dawned on him only when he started practicing, treading the path of sadhana or spiritual discipline. The understanding, which he is now generously sharing with us, was received from the universal library of intuitive knowledge. The emphasis throughout this book, therefore, is on a practical interpretation of the truths of the Mandukya Upanishad for sadhakas (aspirants), not for scholars and academicians.

The Muktiko Upanishad states most categorically that the study of the Mandukya Upanishad, alone, is sufficient for an aspirant to attain liberation. Yet, this is one of the shortest of Upanishads, with only 12 mantras. The profundity of these mantras is cloaked in terse, abstruse language, requiring an interpreter who has reached the other shore of the ocean of samsara. H.H. Swami Rama is uniquely qualified for this task and provides us with a simple, lucid and practical commentary set in the context of the modern world of nuclear technology and nuclear families.

The Mandukya Upanishad tells us in the very first mantra that the imperishable word Om is the whole of the manifested universe. It encompasses all the three divisions of time (past, present and future) as well as that which exists beyond time. In the second mantra, one comes across that Mahavakya (grand saying), "Ayam Atma Brahman", (the Self is verily Brahman) and that all that is manifested is also Brahman. By inference, it is clear that there is complete equivalence between Om, the Self and Brahman.

Swamiji's commentary on these truths is eloquent, touching poetic heights:

> If Om is a symbol,
> It represents all aspects of the universe,
> Manifest and unmanifest;
> If Om is considered a sound,
> The whole universe is its vibration;
> If Om is looked upon as a word,
> It explains all that exists in the universe.

The Mandukya Upanishad tells us that Om, the Self, is the eternal witness of four states of consciousness: the waking, dream and deep sleep states that we are all familiar with, and the fourth state of transcendence, Turiya, in which the sound of Om dissolves into silence, all phenomena cease, duality ends, and tranquility and bliss ensue. One who knows this state knows all, for the individual Self merges into the Universal Self.

The Mandukya Upanishad leads the sadhaka from the waking state, where consciousness is outwardly directed towards gross, material, worldly objects, to the subtler state of dream, where consciousness is inwardly directed to the subtle impressions of worldly experience stored in the subconscious and unconscious mind, and then to the even subtler state of deep sleep in which there is neither dream nor desire and in which the Self revels in the bliss of its own nature. Beyond these 3 states is the fourth state of Turiya.

As stated earlier, Swamiji's interpretation of this Upanishad is for the practical guidance of a sadhaka. In his commentary on the third mantra, dealing with the waking state, Swamiji reminds us that all our learning and degrees cultivate only a very small portion of the mind called the conscious mind. Even with all that education, our conscious mind is not completely in our control. We get caught up in materialistic pursuits and lose sight of our spiritual goal. He gives us a practical strategy for not allowing the world to divert us from the spiritual goal while at the same time escaping the grip of the law of karma. We have to act in the world, there is no choice. We have two options: The first is to use and enjoy the resources of the world as means to an end without getting entangled in the feeling of ownership and doership. We can remain detached while enjoying the gifts of Providence. The other course of action is to attenuate our wants and desires to match our needs, to live with a few necessities, rather than wallowing in worldly comforts that will ensnare us and distract us from the goal. With both options, we have to learn to give away the fruits of our actions, starting first with our immediate families and then learning to expand the circle of love to include all whom we come in touch with.

The fourth mantra deals with the state of dream in which we enjoy the impressions of worldly experiences bubbling up from the unconscious mind, the storehouse of merits and demerits. This state is not in our conscious control. As Swamiji humorously remarks, one cannot join a dream university to become a champion dreamer! However, he gives us practical guidance on how to consciously use introspection and meditation to examine the images rising up from the unconscious and to thus discard what is not useful, the stuff of future distracting dreams. While to a limited extent, dreaming is therapeutic because it deals with unfulfilled desires, it is largely a waste of time. Yogis do not dream! Swamiji also gives us some hints related to the interpretation of the symbolism of dreams. He also counsels therapists to use dream interpretation for helping patients deal with emotions and the four primitive fountains of food, sleep, sexuality and fear.

The fifth mantra describes the state of deep sleep as a blissful state in which there are neither desires nor dreams. The Upanishad also describes this state as an enlightened state (Prajna) in which one can gain more complete understanding of the preceding two states of dream and wakefulness. In his commentary, Swamiji tells us that the bliss of deep sleep is realized only upon waking up and that we are unconscious of this bliss while asleep. Two people go to see a king. One falls asleep while waiting for the king and is unaware of his majestic presence while the other remains awake enjoying the glories of his majesty. This analogy illustrates the difference between the deep sleep state and the state of samadhi. In fact the state of samadhi has also been called a state of sleepless sleep. The technique of yoga nidra allows us to experience this conscious state of sleepless sleep. Yoga nidra provides complete rest for the body, senses, nervous system and mind. Swamiji has given us, (Appendix C of this book), a beautiful and profound kriya (practice) called the Om kriya that will enable us to touch the fringes of samadhi, enjoying the bliss of this state with conscious awareness. Upon regularly and sincerely practicing this kriya, the truths of the sixth mantra will become evident, namely that the experiencer of the three states is the antaryamin, the indwelling controller, the Lord of all, the womb from which all has emerged and into which all returns. Bliss will permeate our minds when we come in touch with this antaryamin.

The seventh mantra gives us a beautiful understanding of the fourth state, Turiya. As with the path of Jnana Yoga (yoga of knowledge) which uses the technique of neti, neti (not this, not this), to proceed towards the Absolute Reality, the mantra starts the process of understanding with negations:

> In Turiya, the consciousness is not inward turned nor outward turned, nor a combination of the two; consciousness is not an undifferentiated mass but it is beyond both cognition and non-cognition. It cannot be known by the senses nor by comparisons or inference; it is intangible and beyond the pale of thought; it is beyond description.

Now where does this leave the sadhaka?! The mantra continues:

> Turiya is the essence of pure consciousness, the real Self, with cessation of all phenomena, tranquil, blissful and one without a second (nondual).

In Mantras 8-11, the Mandukya Upanishad informs us that Om, as a sound, has three component syllables: A, U and M corresponding to the waking, dream and deep sleep states and that there is a fourth soundless component (amatra), corresponding to the transcendent state of Turiya. There is complete equivalence between the component syllables and the states of consciousness. Just as the reverberation of A, merges into U, U into M and M finally merges and dissolves into silence, so too does the waking state lead to the subtler state of dream which yields to the even subtler state of deep sleep which then becomes the gateway to Turiya.

The twelfth and last mantra of the Upanishad echoes the positive characterization of Turiya of the seventh mantra as a state which is blissful, peaceful and nondual. The mantra ends with the declaration:

> Om is verily the Self and he who
> knows this merges into the Universal Self.
> This is to be realized.

The sadhaka is inspired, motivated and filled with hope.

Swamiji, from the vantage point of a realized master, tells us that there is no worldly enjoyment that can compare with the bliss experienced in meditation. Meditation is the only sure way to gain the state of Turiya. Selfless service, prayer and japa are purificatory practices that serve as adjuncts to meditation but the lamp of inner knowledge has to be lit through the practice of meditation. Just as a mountaineer who has successfully scaled the mountain and reached the summit can see the panorama all around the mountain as well as the paths leading upwards and downwards, so the realized sadhaka, upon gaining the summit of Turiya will be simultaneously conscious of the other three states of waking, dreaming and deep sleep while remaining in Turiya.

We are deeply indebted to H.H. Swami Rama for this clear exposition of the profound, inner truths of the Mandukya Upanishad. This book is an edited compilation of a series of lectures delivered many years ago. I was fortunate to be present during these lectures and have used notes of these lectures to present Swamiji's inspired and inspiring commentary on the Mandukya Upanishad. As an editor, I have tried not to come between you and Swamiji by heavy editing, merely to toe the line of rigorous syntax and grammar. I have instead tried to retain the flavour of his spoken word and his charismatic presence. We are indebted to Connie Gage and Wesley van Linda for the engaging cover design, to Kamal (Patrice Hafford) for typesetting this manuscript with meticulous care and to Dr. Ganasan and Mrs. Vijaya Keshaviah for proofreading the manuscript.

This has been a labor of love to express our gratitude to Swamiji for showing us the way. However, as he often reminded us, quoting the Buddha, "Ye light thy own lamp!"

Prakash Keshaviah, Ph.D
Swami Ram Nagar, Dehradun
May 17th, 2007

ॐ

Chapter 1

Introduction

This knowledge which I am giving you has not come through my mind. Some of it is through inner vision or revelation, and the rest through the teachings of the great ones with whom I lived and whose love and blessings I enjoyed. Revelation is that knowledge which flows from the infinite library of the eternal. This knowledge does not come through the senses, or through the mind. This knowledge comes through inner vision and these visions are based on knowledge which is self-evident, which does not need support, which does not need any other evidence.

The knowledge of the Upanishads is called shruti, that which was heard or revealed. These scriptures explain very little and it's difficult to understand them without the right explanation. You won't understand certain words which were used in ancient times. Though the scriptures are very terse, tough, and abstruse in their nature, I am making them easy for you to understand. I learned them so many times; I heard the same scriptures from many, many sages; so I found a way of explaining them in a simple way that you can understand. Otherwise it is said, "Don't teach this vidya, (knowledge) of the Upanishads, to anybody and everybody." I am trying to explain them to you in your own language. Then you will enjoy

1

the subject and know about your individual soul and how the individual soul is related to the cosmic soul, and understand what is moksha, or liberation. Is it possible for us to be liberated? I say, yes, right now!

Let me tell you something. To hear is very good, to hear attentively is even better, but to understand is truly wonderful. To assimilate the knowledge that you are receiving from the scriptures is difficult unless you prepare your mind for that knowledge called para, knowledge from beyond. This knowledge was revealed to the great sages in deep states of contemplation and meditation. It is not wisdom that has come through any human mind. Today, even if you try, you cannot attain that state. During ancient times, the atmosphere, human life, lifestyle, their thinking, austerities and penance, were entirely different. Today's human being is scattered in the external world. Current activities and research are externally and physically oriented offering us many means and comforts. But then, who is enjoying these means and comforts? I do not know. We are not taught to know and understand ourselves, yet we jump into relationships. We live with others; we have to and this just keeps going on. And this sort of education, which does not impart integrated knowledge, does not help us.

When a teacher says something, both the teacher and the student should understand where they are standing as far as consciousness is concerned. What I mean to say is that when we communicate with somebody through words, these words are not understood properly because it's hard to judge from which perspective we are speaking. When Christ was crossing the river Jordan, all his students complained. "Master, you are speaking in parables. We do not understand." During that time his consciousness,

Christ-consciousness, was not towards the teaching, but towards formulating that wisdom which he directly received from the infinite library within.

The Upanishads are called shruti, revelations. You have the Book of Revelation in Christianity, a similar Book of Revelation in Judaism. In fact, there are two Books of Revelation in Judaism which are very similar. And for being chosen for such a great work, you need not be a disciple. If you have studied the Book of Revelation, you know that John, to whom the revelations dawned, was not a disciple, was not one of the 12 apostles. Why was he chosen for the revelations? Why not the disciples who lived close to Christ, for many, many years? It means that every human being has the potential to attain that state, that stature, where he can receive revelations.

This Mandukya Upanishad is the shortest of all Upanishads. It has only 12 verses. It comes from the holy scriptures called the Vedas. It is from the fourth Veda, the Atharva Veda, as is the case with the Mundaka and Prasna Upanishads. In the Muktik-opanishad, it is written, that if one studies only this one Upanishad, the Mandukya Upanishad, one can attain the highest Reality or Absolute Truth, the One without a second. There is no doubt about it. In other Upanishads there are similes used in very mysterious ways. But this Upanishad is very direct, the shortest among all Upanishads, yet profound in its nature.

Many of you have heard the word 'Upanishad,' and many of you have studied and attended a few classes on the Upanishads. The word Upanishad comes from its root 'sad,' which means to loosen, to destroy, and to attain. It has three meanings: that which helps an aspirant to loosen the bonds (of ignorance), that which helps one to destroy the darkness of ignorance, and that which helps one to attain liberation, final liberation. With two prefixes, 'ni' and 'up,' Upanishad means to sit near the teacher, who has been taught in the tradition. And what is that tradition? So far I have not given you the long lineage of the tradition. Today I am going to reveal the names of that eternal tradition.

One who goes to the highest shrine of India in the Himalayas called Badrinath, will see that, at Joshimath, there is a point where two mountains are visible. One is called Nara, the perfect human being, the other is called Narayana, the absolute representative of Brahman. These two mountains, called Nara and Narayana, stand facing each other. The mountain Nara is lower in height than Narayana. Now it has been recorded by the Survey of India that these two mountains are shrinking, coming closer together. In 80 years, the distance between Nara and Narayana has reduced by about 14 inches. All the Himalayas are shrinking; they are not very ancient mountains. Over 80 years they have shrunk six inches. The higher of these two mountains is considered to represent Narayana, the representative of the Absolute, who knew the wisdom of the Vedas, and taught his disciple Nara, who is also known as Brahmadeva.

So, from where does the lineage of our tradition flow? The first is Brahmadeva, the lotus-born one. Then comes Vashishtha, Lord Rama's guru. This surely indicates that the tradition is older than the Ramayana. After Vashishtha comes Shakti, then Parasara, followed by Vyasa, author of the epic Mahabharata, and then Shuka. Up to the seventh generation, there was a father and son lineage. The father initiated his first son and thus the teachings continued, were perpetuated. But after that comes the guru-disciple lineage with Gaudapada, who was Adi Shankaracharya's grandguru, that is guru's guru.

Gaudapada wrote a commentary on the Mandukya Upanishad called Mandukya Karika. That's my favorite book. This book was taught to me by my master and other teachers in the Himalayas. In the monastic order, if someone has not learnt this scripture, he does not know anything. He's not considered to be intelligent, he's not considered to be a teacher, he's not considered to be a brilliant person. I studied it 22 times, and yet I did not understand. But once I started practicing, then I started to understand. This commentary of 200 verses on the 12 verses of the Mandukya Upanishad is the finest of all commentaries and of all books of Vedantic philosophy. It is believed that Narayana revealed that knowledge to Gaudapada, inspiring him to write the Karika. The Karika is the most terse, abstruse and difficult scripture in Vedantic literature, nay, in the library of man. Shankaracharya then wrote a tika, another commentary, on Gaudapadacharya's commentary. The 12 verses of the Mandukya Upanishad were thus expanded, becoming voluminous. In India it took me 91 days to explain the Karika.

Imagine an equilateral triangle. Life is exactly like that equilateral triangle. If one of the angles is disturbed, the equilateral triangle will be disturbed. There is no integration in our lives today, and that is why we are not perfect human beings, perfect nara. We will get teachers like Narayana and Gaudapadacharya only if we become good nara, good human beings. Here, according to the Upanishadic philosophy, a good human being means one who has learned how to integrate body, mind, and heart: healthy body, a sound mind, and a good heart. Only physical muscles will not make us healthy human beings. An intellectual gymnasium alone, will not help us, nor will only emotional development (heart) help us. We need to understand integration of body, mind and heart. When we try to analyze something intellectually, we put our emotions aside. We do not understand our emotions and we say that our emotions make us blind. That's not true! Emotion is a great power! If we know and understand how to direct that power, it can lead us to the heights of ecstasy in a moment's time. You cannot depend on the intellect alone, because it gathers its data from the external world, which is subject to change, death, and decay. That which goes through change, death and decay changes its form all the time. This is the data that is being gathered by the mind, by the intellect, which is never purified, which has no support of the disciplined faculties of mind. Therefore, our data collection does not help us, does not lead us.

Mandukya Upanishad, though the shortest of all Upanishads, is a most revered, profound Upanishad that teaches us how to know four states of consciousness: the waking, dreaming and sleeping states, and Turiya, the fourth state, beyond the first three. What is the waking state? What is the difference between dreaming and waking states? In the dreaming state, why do all things change, get distorted? You say, the dreaming state is true as long as it lasts. How about the waking state? Is it any more real than the dream state? What is deep sleep actually? Why do you go to deep sleep? Why do you need sleep? When you are in deep sleep, nothing is true. But if you go to Turiya, you will realize that Turiya alone is the truth.

The first state is the waking state. What happens to us when we remain awake? Our education actually teaches us how to cultivate this waking state alone. Our education does not teach us how to dream. That portion of mind which dreams, is not cultivated by us, is not under our conscious control. So, look at the shallowness of this education that we receive and the way we are taught. We rely so much on these dark words; they can never give us light. It's not possible, because darkness cannot produce light! And our whole life is spent in this darkness. Dark words, we read them; we read what others say and we become opinionated. We learn how to form opinions based on the opinions of others, but that is not profound knowledge. The dreaming portion of mind and the sleeping portion of mind are not under our conscious control. That which is cultivated by us is merely the waking state of mind. Our entire educational system helps us in utilizing only that portion of mind which functions during the waking state. How does sleep help you? Why is sleep so close to death? Why are you terrified by death, even by merely hearing the word death? What happens to you when you die? Is your personality, your being, completely annihilated? Or do you live even after death? Are you reborn? Is there any logical proof that when a human being departs from this world, he still lives? The fourth state, which is called the state of Turiya, is the highest state that can be attained. It is beyond samadhi. Samadhi is a state of mind; Turiya is a state of consciousness.

In this Upanishad, there is a unique combination of psychology and profound philosophy; a clear exposition and understanding of the four states of consciousness. What is actually this waking state? When we are awake, our senses function. The moment we awaken, our mind employs the senses, the senses contact the world of objects, and thus we perceive things of the external world. Is this waking state a reality? According to this Upanishad, no! It too is like a dream. When you go to sleep, before you reach deep sleep where there is no mental content, you go through a state that is called the dreaming state. How is that dreaming reality similar to this waking reality? According to this book, and according to the commentators, both are unreal, both are illusions. The way you perceive this world and worldly objects, is not how it really is. You are a simple, normal human being, but in your dream, you can become a king or president of a country for a few hours, as long as you are dreaming. Suppose you are really a king, or president of a country, but you dream that you have become a donkey. For a few hours, you become a donkey, even though you are a president! This Upanishad explains that the waking reality is no more real than the dreaming reality. This scripture says that if the dreaming state is not real, then the waking state is also not real. They both are unreal, because when you go to deep sleep they both lose their existence.

Does the world lose its existence if you do not perceive it with your senses? Of course! Suppose you don't use one of the senses, say the eyes, the world would be different. This world appears the way you see it because of your senses. We all have similar senses, which is why we have similar experiences. Suppose you develop a sixth sense, the world would look different. The horizon that I see through this window is very narrow and limited. I cannot convince a person who is outside the room that the horizon is so small. He will laugh at me. I cannot convince the person who is in darkness, who has never seen light, anything about light. I cannot convince a person without the sense of taste, who has been eating sweets, about what sweet taste is. There are some things which are inexplicable, they can be realized, they can be experienced, but they cannot be explained.

In the world, if you say there is peace, it means there is no war. A gap between two wars is called peace in the world. Peace is a relative term. But that's not what we want. We want a peace, tranquility, which lasts forever, as long as we live. Which part of our self needs peace? Our body needs rest, not peace. Our senses do not need peace. There is one verse explained in Kathopanishad. Listen to this, *Yada panchavatishthante jnanani manasa saha buddhischa na vicheshtate tamahuh parmam gatim.* When my five senses are not distracted, my mind is calm; during that time I am in a state of tranquility. So when your senses are not distracted, not dissipated, when your mind is tranquil, during that time you attain a state that is called the state of samadhi. Samadhi is that state where there is no question in your mind. Is it possible for you or your mind to attain that state where there is no question? Not possible? But there is a way! If you forget the languages in which your mind jabbers all the time, if you know the unlearning method, which is not taught in any school, then you can attain that state. That is possible and can be proved scientifically. You have a glass of water. You are asked to empty it. You have emptied the glass of water. Still that glass is not empty because there is now air in it. How will you empty it of air? By filling it. So is the case with the mind. First you will have to drain the gross aspects of your mind and then you will have to fill your mind to get rid of that which is called ancient dirt in our minds. That is why methods like japa, meditation and prayer are recommended.

According to Vedanta, one of the schools of Indian philosophy, the easiest way, the shortest cut of all, is to cut your ego and you are there. But it's difficult to cut your ego. When you try to cut your ego, when you want to expand the horizon of your mind, you will feel afraid, afraid of seeing your personality being dissolved. When a drop of water merges into the ocean, it does not lose its identity. It becomes the ocean. A time comes, a plateau comes, when a meditator or contemplator thinks that individuality is being threatened. He's insecure because he does not know what is happening, does not know what is going to happen in the future.

I want to pose a question. A black cow eats green grass, produces white milk, which turns into yellow butter. What do you have to say about it? How does it happen? Physics has not gone into such things in great detail because it deals only with the external world. What I mean to say is that there are many things beyond our grasp, many things beyond the field of our intellectualization. If you systematically pursue, enquire and explore, you can attain the fourth state. Nowhere else has this subject matter been discussed before in this way, except in the Mandukya Upanishad. Nowhere else, has there been a detailed commentary like the Karika of Gaudapada Acharya, which is respected by Hindus, Buddhists, and by all the intellectuals of the world.

Our individual soul creates bondage because of attachment. This way we are caught in a snare of bondages . We want to be free from all these bondages, for freedom is one thing that we all yearn for. Freedom will give us happiness. If we are not free, we can never be happy. If we say that it's after all God's creation, God has made us this way, that is not enough. Why should God, the Lord of equality, have such discrimination? Then we are at the mercy of God. You cannot do anything because it's all God's grace, whatever you do. You cannot change, you cannot improve. So the right philosophy says, no! A human being is an unfinished being and has the opportunity to complete himself or herself, and can attain wisdom in this lifetime by right understanding and by practicing that which is understood. One must learn this scripture. Nowhere does this scripture talk about God, about any deity. It talks about three states of consciousness and leads you to attain the fourth state. Let me tell you that this scripture has nothing to do with any religion. Nowhere is any religion, any faith, accepted or condemned. We are not here to discuss religion and which religion is good and which is bad. All the religions are one and the same. We are here to understand the profound teachings of the Mandukya Upanishad which can lead us to understand, analyze, and then finally realize the highest peak of life, the summit of life called Turiya.

ॐ

Chapter 2

Om, a Symbol, a Sound, a Word

First Mantra

हरिः ओम् । ओमित्येतदक्षरमिदं सर्वं
तस्योपव्याख्यानं भूतं भवद्भविष्यदिति
सर्वमोङ्कार एव । यच्चान्यत् त्रिकालातीतं
तदप्योङ्कार एव ॥ १ ॥

*Harih Om. Om-ity-etad-aksharam-idam
sarvam tasyopavyakhyanam bhutam bhavad
bhavishyad-iti sarvam omkara eva. Yaccanyat
trikalatitam tad apy omkara eva.*

The Mandukya Upanishad starts with, *"Harih
Om. Om-ity-etad aksharam-idam sarvam."*
The entire universe is the syllable Om.

Om is the eternal sound. In the Bible it is also
said, "In the beginning was the Word, and the Word
was with God and the Word was God." And what
was that Word? That Word was Om, because there
is only one sound that can be produced by opening
the lips as well as by keeping them closed. With your

lips closed, if you hum any sound of any language, it will come out as Om. Om is made up of A, U and M. A comes from the throat, from our vocal cords. U rolls down the palate, and M comes when you seal your lips. All sounds are therefore derived from Om. All mantras originate from Om.

If Om is a symbol, it represents all aspects of the universe, manifest and unmanifest. If Om is considered to be a sound, the whole universe is its vibration. Every sound creates a form. When I clap my hands, that sound will vibrate and create a particular form. The vibration of Om creates, as its form, the entire universe. If Om is looked upon as a word, this word explains all that exists in the universe. All potentialities, forms and thoughts are expressions of Om. The entire Upanishadic teaching is condensed in the knowledge of Om. He, who knows Om both theoretically and practically, through experience, knows all.

Tasyopavyakhyanam bhutam bhavad bhavishad-iti sarvam omkara eva.
The following is the exposition of Om. Everything in the past, present, and future is verily Om.

Om can show you how to come out of the conditionings of your mind called past, present, and future. It's difficult to comprehend the present. We all know about the past, how our past thinking, actions and emotions make a space in the depths of our consciousness, in the unconscious mind, where they live for a long time. They live there forever and ever, unless you know how to deal with them. They live in that reservoir of merits and demerits. You have to know how to approach your unconscious mind and you have to know how to deal with the un-conscious impressions.

This Upanishad helps us to understand the prime conditionings of our mind, which are mainly three — time, space, and causation. What is time? How does time control our mind? What is space, what is causation? Once we understand these, then we can free our mind from them. Let me tell you something. No matter how much you concentrate your mind, no matter how much you meditate and contemplate, it will not help you if you have not understood time, space and causation, which create the conditionings of your mind. If your mind is conditioned, no matter how you deal with it, it is a conditioned mind. That's why knowledge is important. If you do not have knowledge, your actions will not be useful. If I am looking at the sun but I am walking backwards, will I ever reach there? Therefore we have to understand the conditionings of our mind. And without profound knowledge, the conditionings cannot be known. And without knowing the conditionings, we can have a concentrated mind but we cannot have mental freedom. Therefore, it is very important to understand the conditionings of the mind, and to then free the mind of these conditionings.

I will give you an example. Look at my two fingers. Now there is a space between them; the two have created a space. Now if there is no space, there will be no time, there will be no conditioning. So you can become free when you have profound knowledge of Advaita, nonduality, One absolute without a second. Without this knowledge, you cannot be free. You can make your mind one-pointed, inward, but you cannot get freedom from the conditionings of your mind. So the prime conditionings of your mind should be understood and systematically dealt with. Then, such a mind will have the power to penetrate into the deeper folds of your being. It's a systematic journey which goes from gross to subtle, to the subtler and then the subtle-most aspect of your life. It's a very interesting journey! I don't know why people say that it's difficult. I think logically it should be very easy. You may get lost in the external world, but you can never be lost within yourself. It's difficult to find something in the external world because there are many disturbances. It's very easy to find something within because there are fewer disturbances. From where do disturbances enter our system? From the external world. When we learn to understand our relationship with the external world, that is, this waking reality, and learn to deal with it, we will never allow the waking reality and its distractions to create a groove in our minds and hearts. Once we understand that the path of the self is simple, easy and natural, and that it's our birthright, then our desires will start flowing inwards instead of outwards to the external world. Can we live by living within only? No. We have to learn to create a bridge between within and without. The outside world gives us means and comforts. So those means satisfy and help that part of us which needs these comforts.

Yaccanyat trikalatitam tad apy omkara eva.
That which is beyond time, space, and causation is also Om.

It means that there is a fourth step, fourth state of consciousness, which is beyond these three states. That's called amatra, the soundless state of Om. It's like the top of the mountain from where you can see up, down, here, there and everywhere. From Turiya, you can see what dreaming is like, from where you allow dreams to come. You will see how dreams are being formulated. You can watch your dreaming states, it's very interesting. You can even watch your sleeping state and yet remain fully awake. You are in deep sleep, yet you can remain fully awake. It can be done if you learn yoga nidra. If you are able to do it consciously, it is called sleepless sleep.

Unless you learn how to sit, how to breathe, how to have coordinated mind and how to go beyond and then put yourself into absolute sound and then absolute silence, you will never understand that. This inward process can be practiced by all of us, but we hardly make efforts to do that. First of all, since our childhood, we are not trained to do that. No one teaches us how to sit still, how to breathe in a serene way, how to be calm.

Second mantra

सर्वं ह्येतद् ब्रह्म, अयमात्मा ब्रह्म,
सोऽयमात्मा चतुष्पात् ॥ २ ॥

Sarvam hy-etad brahma ayam-atma brahma soyam-atma chatuspat.

Sarvam hy-etad brahma ayam-atma brahma
All this, whatsoever is seen here, there, and everywhere, is Brahman. This very Self, Atman, is Brahman, the Absolute Reality.

Tell me, is there any space, is there any place where there is no Brahman, where there is no ultimate reality? Brahman is the Supreme Consciousness. There is no difference between Atman, the individual Self and Brahman, the Universal Self. As the sages of the Upanishads have taught, "Tat tvam asi." That thou art. First of all, you should understand yourself on three levels. The perishable self, which is termed as mere self, is made up of the body, senses, breath and conscious mind; the semi-immortal self is your unconscious mind along with the individual soul or jivatma. The immortal part is the Self or Atman. When you drop this body, that is, when the vital pranas have departed from the body, that which remains is called the unconscious mind. The unconscious mind is a vehicle for the individual soul. It is the storehouse of merits and demerits and contains many sorts of desires and aspirations. These desires again lead us back to this world, because we have unfulfilled desires. And for fulfilling these desires you come back again and again. I am not confusing you; I am not telling you to believe in reincarnation; but there is no other way. You cannot accomplish the entire life's work, so much work, in such a short time. Not possible!

You are called an individual because you are enjoying this vehicle, you are driving this vehicle, you own this vehicle called the unconscious mind. If you were to break the walls of this hall, then there will be no hall, this will all be one horizon. This super-imposition that we have a hall, separates the space within this hall from the space outside. Similarly, in Turiya, the fourth state, you drop that vehicle, that which makes you an individual, and you merge with the universal, become one with the center of consciousness. You experience great joy. There is a final meeting of the individual or Atman with Brahman, the Universal. That final meeting is called Turiya, the fourth state. This Upanishad says that you have to experience this state; you have to understand, that there is only one experiencer of the waking, dream and sleep states, and that in Turiya, the fourth state, you become one with that experiencer.

So when you see how that center of consciousness gradually goes through evolution, when we understand how we have come to the world, to the waking state, then we can go back through the same process to the center of consciousness. The question arises, what good is that? Why do you want to attain that? What is the necessity? Why do teachers talk about it and why do students want to know about that state? What will happen to us? Well, we will be transformed. We will attain the goal of life, this human aspiration, which we all want to attain, namely, perfection. That perfection will come when we will go back to the source of consciousness, to the source of wisdom, to the source of the eternal, and that's what we all want. And we want it in this lifetime. We don't want to postpone it for the next life. We should not postpone it! Most of us think that enlightenment, or meeting God, or becoming perfect, or attaining samadhi is very difficult. That cannot be, that's not true. Is it difficult to meet yourself? Do you need anyone's help to meet yourself? Do you need anyone's support to meet yourself? Do you have to lean on someone to meet yourself?

Soyam-atma chatuspat.
This Atman has four aspects.

What are the four aspects? They are aspects of consciousness. Three of the states are those experienced during waking, dreaming and deep sleep and the fourth is a state beyond. Consciousness experienced in the first three states is known as Apara-

Brahman, whereas, consciousness of the fourth state is Para-Brahman, the transcendent Reality. When an aspirant tears through the veil of Maya or ignorance, he understands that the universe is an illusion and that the fourth state of Turiya is the only Reality. He realizes that the individual Atman and the universal Brahman are one and the same.

The sages of the Upanishads have referred to Om as setu or bridge, bridging the chasm between the individual and the Universal. The Yoga Sutras state, *Tasya vachaka Brahman*, that is, Om is the designator, the signpost, pointing to Brahman. In another Upanishad, a simile is used: Om is the bow, Atman the arrow and Brahman, the target.

In this Upanishad, A represents the waking state, U, the dreaming state and M, the sleeping state. But beyond them, there is a silent state which is called Turiya, the fourth state, which is beyond these three states. The experience of waking merges into the subtler state of dreaming, which in turn, merges into the even subtler state of deep, dreamless sleep, and ultimately, deep sleep merges into Turiya, the fourth transcendent state.

In chanting Om, A merges into U, which merges into M, and finally dissolves into silence. That's called amatra, the soundless state of Om. It's easy to understand this with a simile: You stand on the banks of the Ganges, or any river, and you hear the sound of the river. You may think that if you follow the flow of the river upstream, you will find how and from where that sound has originated. Finally, you arrive at the source and you'll find that there, there is no sound at all. All sounds verily come from that place where there is no sound, that is, from silence.

ॐ
Chapter 3

The Waking Consciousness, Vaishvanara

Mantra 3

जागरितस्थानो बहिष्प्रज्ञः सप्ताङ्ग
एकोनविंशतिमुखः स्थूलभुग्
वैश्वानरः प्रथमः पादः ॥ ३ ॥

*Jagarita-sthano bahish-prajnah saptanga
ekonavimshati mukhah sthula bhug vaishvanarah
prathama padah*

*Jagarita-sthano ... vaishvanarah prathama
padah*
**The waking state, Vaishvanara, is the first
aspect.**

These states are not states of mind, they are not
creations of the mind and they are not projections of
the mind. Mind has very little to do with your waking
state or dreaming state. These are states of consciousness.

*bahish-prajnah saptanga ekonavimshati
mukhah sthula bhug*

Consciousness is turned to the external and experiences gross objects through seven instruments and nineteen channels.

What are those 7 instruments? There are 5 elements, namely, earth, water, fire, air and space. These five along with breath and ego make up seven instruments. Then, what are the nineteen channels? If we add the five cognitive senses (sight, hearing, smell, touch and taste), the five active senses, (speech, grasping, walking, reproduction and elimination), the 5 pranas (prana, apana, samana, vyana and udana) and the four aspects of the inner instrument or antahakarana (mind, ego , intellect and the storehouse of memories) we get nineteen channels. When we understand their functions well, we know how consciousness experiences the external world and what the limitations of a human being are when he experiences only one aspect of consciousness, directed towards the phenomenal world in the waking state.

During the waking state, how does your mind function? The waking state is not a projection of your mind, remember that. All the objects in the external world are definitely projections of shakti, the power of consciousness, but the waking state is not a product of your mind. So how do mind and waking state relate with each other? That small part of the totality of mind which functions during the waking state is called the conscious mind; it is not the unconscious mind. If it becomes unconscious mind, then there will be no waking state.

The Upanishads say that first you will have to face the external world. You will have to learn the technique of doing your duties in the external world. If you know how to live in the external world, perhaps the external world will not create any barriers on the path of unfoldment. Can the external world help you in attaining the goal of life? Yes and no, both. If the external world does not create problems for you, then it is helpful. If external world creates problems for you, then it's impossible for you to progress on the path of unfoldment. I am here, now. If you all decide that Swamiji should not meditate, I cannot, for you will kick me from this side, give me a blow from the other side, creating hindrances for me. How can I meditate? So, external world can create barriers for you. If the barriers are not there, it is a great help.

When Alexander the Great invaded India, his teacher asked him to bring back two things—the flute and the scripture called the Bhagavad Gita. So after conquering a part of India, he told his prime minister, "I want to meet a swami, a wise man, because the flute and Gita will be of no use if there is no swami." The minister went in search of a wise man. He asked the people around and someone said, "Such and such a person, sitting on that mountain is a wise man and he will help you, sir." That wise man was sitting on a rock. Alexander approached him and said, "What can I do for you, sir?" He smiled, but did not look at Alexander. So the prime minister said, "He's Alexander the Great. Perhaps you do not know that he's a very great man of the world, a very famous warrior who conquered the whole world." The wise man would not look at him. So again Alexander asked, "What can I do for you, sir?" He replied, "Just remove yourself, let the sunlight shine on me. That's what you can do."

What can you do for others? If you do not create any barrier, any hindrance, any problem for others, that is a great help. This is my point. When you go out to help somebody, perhaps your selfishness and ego are mingled, and that will not help. Don't create barriers, hindrances and obstacles for others; let them grow. Let them unfold; let them tread the path of light. That is the greatest help that you can give. It's called minding your own business!

All the things in the world have a name and form. Is there any form that does not go through change, death and decay? So name and form are temporary aspects of that something which goes on changing. There is one word in Sanskrit for this world, samsara. It continues, goes on, like a river that goes on flowing. One mass of water passes, yet another mass comes, fills that gap and there is no gap at all. There is continuity. We will all go away, others will come. There will be continuity. This world will always remain crowded, over-crowded. So, this is the world, this is samsara. Now this external aspect of samsara, of this universe, is called Vaishvanara.

Herein lies a secret for the sadhaka, the aspirant. To turn the consciousness within, you will have to use a method of withdrawing the senses from the external world. That is called sparsa yoga, yoga of touch. If you analyze two things in your life, one called pain and another called pleasure, you will come to know that pain and pleasure, these two stimuli, are received when your senses contact matter. The Gita explains it this way, *Matra sparshastu kaunteya sheetoshna sukha dukha da*. You feel pain and pleasure, heat and cold because your senses contact the objects of the external world. If you can stop doing this, you will not feel pain or pleasure; you will not feel heat or cold. So all the time, with the help of your senses, you are in contact with the objects of the external world. You do not know how to withdraw your senses. That is why on the eight runged ladder of yoga, ashtanga yoga, the fifth rung, pratyahara or sensory withdrawal, is very important. There are no books on the subject of pratyahara. There are books on concentration, there are books on meditation, there are books on samadhi, but there are no books on pratyahara, because it's a practical technique. You should learn to withdraw your senses, to turn inward, because the senses make you contact the external world and that's why you feel pain and pleasure. You have to be free from pain and pleasure; you can be free!

There was a swami who fell down from the mountains. These are not mere stories, they are true, I assure you. Three of his bones were broken. I took him to the doctor, Dr. Mukherji, a surgeon, who is still alive and lives in Varanasi. The doctor said, "I want to give you anesthesia." He said, "What is that?" He did not know what it was. The doctor said, "It's a gas-like substance which will lead you to a state where there will be no pain." The swami said, "It's easy for me to withdraw my senses. How long will it take for you to perform the operation?" The doctor said, "Half an hour." He said, "Are you sure you can do your job within half an hour? If you need more time, let me know now." The doctor said, "O.k., give me 40 minutes." The swami said, "I give you 50 minutes." And within a second he composed himself, withdrew his consciousness from that limb, and the doctor began the operation. It took him exactly 50 minutes. After 50 minutes, the swami suddenly smiled, the operation was over. How could he do this? Because he practiced pratyahara. He did not allow his mind to use the sensory channels which distract and dissipate the power of mind and lead it to the external world. These are agents that the mind employs to contact the external world. But whose power is that? Is it the power of the mind? Is it the power of the senses? No. It's the power of consciousness. The mind, senses and other channels are all using the power of consciousness. When you learn to train your mind through which this power flows to the external world, by separating it from the senses, by not employing the senses, then that state is called the state of conscious withdrawal, which is very important for meditation.

Let us discuss Vaishvanara, the gross world, world outside of us, the external world. How should we deal with the external world, and if not properly dealt with, how does it affect our inner situation, inner condition? How do we strengthen our attachment to the things of the world which are fleeting fast, which are moving, which are subject to change, death and decay? What should our attitude be towards the external world? We have to live in this world. Let us analyze how to live in the external world.

First we need to have a concept. Unless we build a solid concept, we cannot be successful. So all our concepts should be filtered well, and we should have a personal philosophy which does not create barriers for us in our search for enlightenment. We have to understand that. That concept should be built first. What should that concept be? Without a concept, even if we do good deeds, they will not be very helpful to us, will not be of much use to us. You see today, the morality of human beings is being preserved by the government. Remove the army and police force, and next day you will find that fifty percent of human beings have been killed. There will be a lot of chaos. So if the gun is still controlling human destiny, it means that we are still primitive. It means we are not aware of other human beings around us; we don't have love for others. We don't even have love for ourselves, we are selfish beings. We are called talking animals. Therefore, we have to understand that, individually, we all have a responsibility for creating a good atmosphere around us by understanding our own self. In the external world, karma seems to be an inevitable law. There is no dispute about this. Science and religion hardly meet. Philosophy, religion, and science never meet. But here on the basis of this universal law, called the law of karma (action), science, religion and philosophy, all three meet, and say with one voice, "As you sow, so shall you reap." It's a law. Every action has its reaction; science says that. When you try to understand the cause, then you will come to know that it's not something mysterious. You can shape your whole life. You can guide your whole life towards your goal. It depends on whether you have built your philosophy or not. You are all thinkers, but you have not built your philosophy. Philosophy of individual life is one of the padas or quarters that is explained in this Mandukya Upanishad. We'll discuss that.

If you are the president of a great country, what will happen? You will find that you are inside a jail. This is not a good sign. I've seen it in my country. I went to see a minister, like a Secretary in your country. His whole house was surrounded by gunmen. I said, "I pity this man." He was very close to me and, earlier, when I used to see him, there was no guard, nobody, and I used to drive my car straight up to his front door. But now a policeman stopped me. He said, "Who are you? Do you have any appointment?" I said, "I don't need an appointment, he's a very good friend of mine." He said, "No, no, no, you have to have an appointment." I said, "Go and talk to him." He said, "No." He wouldn't allow me to meet my friend, the minister. I telephoned my friend. It took him 7 days to give me an appointment. By that time I had left for Rishikesh. What a miserable situation we create for ourselves. We are not living in a nice world, I tell you. I thought that the world would be free from wars after the Second World War, because I remember what happened in the Second War. But I think, now, there is war in every home. Homes were peaceful before, 50 years earlier. Now there is turmoil in every home, there is divorce in every home, there is misunderstanding in every home. Everybody is irresponsible.

A human being is responsible for his own actions. It means he has power to do and to undo, to direct all his resources and energy towards his goal. Can action lead you to Brahman, the final goal? No, it's not possible. There is not a single action that can lead you to attaining the highest. Well then, why are we doing actions? Because we cannot live without acting. And if we do not perform our duties, the call of duties will create barriers for us and then we cannot get anywhere. We have to do our duties. Is there any way that we can do our duties, yet remain free? We have to find that way.

First of all let us try to understand the external world, Vaishvanara. We have to learn to understand how a human being functions in the world. What is that law we are talking of? For a common man it is hard to understand that he can never live without doing actions. Even if you renounce your home and all that you have, yet you have to perform actions. You are not like a dry leaf being swept by the wind making certain figures in space. You are a human being. Before you do any action, there is a thought. Your thought is virtually action in the subtle world. Before a tree grows, before the seed sprouts, it already germinates in the subtle world. So when you talk about karma, you should know that your karma, your action, is virtually a thought, a thought mingled with emotion, a thought mingled with doubt, a thought mingled with desire and want. I like to do something. There is no intensity in my liking. When I have to do it, it means that I have, within myself, decided to do something with all my might.

So when you are doing actions, there comes another step. That next step is called duty. Who gives you this duty that you are talking of today? You waste your whole life in the name of duty. "Why are you going home? Stay, take rest, relax." "No, I have to go home, this is my duty." You always talk about your duty. Your life is duty-oriented, duty towards your people. But who created these duties for you? You assumed these duties. By nature, you assume duties: this is my duty, this is not my duty. Then you act according to your assumption. You assume certain duties and you work hard to accomplish those duties. But those duties are assumed by you. Now, in this whole universe, only human beings are responsible for duties. An animal is not responsible for doing its duty. Why do we human beings take responsibility for doing our duties? Because, in the cycle of evolution, which is revolving without any problem, without any hindrance, a stage comes when you become a human being. You are responsible, then, to do your duties. We all function according to our duties. We do karmas. In other worlds, like the animal world, the animal is doing its duty, but the animal is being controlled by Nature, while a human being is not controlled by Nature. He has his free will, he assumes his duties. An animal is not responsible for anything because the animal is not free.

Now you have two things. Firstly, you have to do your duty with full responsibility, being conscious of the idea that you cannot live without doing your duty. You have to do the duties you have assumed. Before you were born in a particular family, the family was there, the society was there, the country was there, the nation was there. What is your duty? Your duty, first, is to your people at home, for home is a nucleus and society is its expansion. Great scriptures, like the Bhagavad Gita, say that you can renounce your personal duties for the sake of serving your society. You can renounce the duties you perform for your household if you have expanded yourself and assumed the responsibility that you have to serve society. You can renounce society for serving your nation. You can renounce your nation for serving the whole of humanity. You can renounce the whole of humanity only for the service of the Lord. This is also personal evolution. But as human beings, we all should know the law of karma first, if we are trying to understand Vaishvanara, the external world, the gross world, the world we perceive with our senses.

How to perform our duties towards the people around us, towards our nation? There should be no disagreement between performance of our duties and the purpose of life. Don't forget this. Conflict comes when you indulge too much in the world, forgetting the aim of life. The aim of life is not to experience only one aspect of life. How to live in the external world is only one aspect of life. What is the art of living in the external world? If you are skilled, you can be successful, but you are not complete.

Now here arises a problem. You want to be successful in the external world, but what success means is not properly interpreted. Suppose you have two million dollars and others do not have that much; if you have five houses and others have only one house, do you think that is success, that is progress? For many of you it is progress and you are very successful. But this success is not a very healthy success for you because your success is not related to the goal of your life. What is your goal of life? Perhaps you are forgetting the goal of life.

There is one intoxication which is greater than any other intoxication, greater than intoxication for liquor, for marijuana, or any other drug. And that intoxication is workaholism, a heavy intoxication. It's directly related to the ego, where you do not know and you do not understand what you are doing. I have seen a father who had four children, and three children did not know him. By chance one day, when he was sleeping, one of the children got up, and said, "Mama, who is this man sleeping next to you?" He used to come home late every night, and he used to leave his home early in the morning. Work, work, work. When you enter into self-created competition, you may achieve something, status in society, but you are really wasting that skill that you are using to attain that status. You are not taking care of the goal of your life. So any action that you perform should not oppose the main philosophy of your life. This should be considered, because functioning in the external world is only a small aspect of your life.

Now, how should you function? You will realize when helplessness comes, one after another. You cannot live without doing action, and you have to perform the action, and when you perform the action, you are bound to reap the fruits of your action. Your dream is your dream, my dream is my dream. Now those fruits which you reap every day, inspire you to do more actions. This way you are caught in a whirlpool and you cannot come out of it. You want to come out, but you cannot. You, yourself, have created this whirlpool. You are performing actions, then reaping the fruits, which in turn inspire you to do more actions; this goes on your whole life, till the very last breath of your life. You always think of only one thing, what is good action? Good, means according to your convenience, and for your own benefit. You forget what is good for others. You forget that other human beings are like you. You completely ignore that part. So you isolate yourself from the whole and start building your ego, your individuality. You can become a great egotist and a great individual, but then you cannot be enlightened. We feel helpless because we cannot live without performing our duties.

The best method of using the waking state, the conscious part of your mind, is by being conscious of the things you are doing. Don't do what you do not want to do. If you force yourself, that could be injurious for you, because after you have done the action, you will repent. So don't do it unless you are fully convinced that it should be done by you, that it is good for you, it is beneficial for you. Otherwise, don't do it.

Learning to do your actions and duties selflessly, skillfully, and lovingly, that is the only way to get freedom from the bondage of karma. But there are other bondages created by other states of mind and other states of consciousness. Remember that states of mind are different from states of consciousness. Waking, dreaming, sleeping are the states of consciousness; pain, pleasure and the like are states of mind; the two are entirely different.

You cannot convince yourself to do voluntary, selfless service unless you have understood the bondage of karma fully, in all times, past, present, and future. It's not possible, because your samskaras, the impressions of past actions stored in your unconscious mind, will motivate you to do selfish work and selfish deeds, which create snares and entanglements. You can be free from the past karmas, by transforming yourself. Once you are transformed, you are free from the past karmas.

Now you have all heard of charity. Charity is considered to be the finest of all actions. You are doing charitable work, but if you are doing charitable work egotistically, with the motivation that others will adore you, revere you, call you great because you are doing something good, then, that is not charitable work. Many people do charitable work to satisfy their egotistical whims, desire for name and fame. Many people do charity because they have been told that if you do something here, then in the next life you will get something there. But a fortunate few do charity for the right reason. "Well, I am hoarding so much money, hoarding is not good. What right do I have to deprive others and hoard? Let me renounce all this for the good of others." When this feeling comes, when this thought comes, when you understand this formula, then you start doing charity. Such charity is definitely helpful on the path of unfoldment, on the path of enlightenment. Then you understand, "I cannot live without doing actions. It's a must. I have to reap the fruits of my actions. This is also true; but I have to offer the fruits of my actions to others, otherwise my actions will create bondage for me."

So what is the law? The law is giving. Law of life is giving, not taking. And that's what you call love. The moment you understand that the real key to action and duty is love, then you are free. You do your duties with love and you are free. Then there will be no stress. Why is the world so stressed today? Because we are all functioning mechanically, like robots. All our research is materially-oriented research, finally leading to discontent. We lose all that we have, and acquire that which we do not need, namely, stress. We form habits which are very injurious for us. They are our own deeds. And do you know how powerful habits are? If you analyze them you'll realize that your habits will affect you even after death. You don't go to hell or heaven, but you remain in your own habit patterns. Many of you believe that you go to hell or heaven. There is no such office which assigns you to hell or heaven. According to your actions, you create habit patterns and you remain in these habit patterns even after death. Any action performed without love is injurious for human growth.

Now, what is that love? That which leads you to the next step of life, freedom from the bondage of karma in the external world. You have to learn to be free because you are constantly creating bondages for yourself, and you cannot help it. You have to do actions, you have to do your duties, and you have to reap the fruits of your duties, and those duties enslave you. You are the slave of your duties, accept it! How to be free? Unless you learn to do your duty effectively, skillfully, freely, lovingly, and happily, you cannot understand the mystery. And it can be understood in one second's time. "Well, I cannot live without doing my duties. I have to, because I am a human being. Let me learn to offer the fruits of my actions to others." Others, means whom? Not strangers, nobody does that. Offer the fruits to the people with whom you live, your family members. We should understand that we are all part of one family. If all of us learn and decide that we will work for each other, everyone will be free. I am working for you; I am not in bondage. You are working for me; you are not in bondage. There will be harmony. The home in which you live is a miniature universe, a training ground where you learn how to be free from the laws of the universe. You are only dealing with the gross aspect of life, Vaishvanara, in the first state. You have not attained anything as yet. This makes you aware that learning to do your duty effectively, skillfully, freely, lovingly and happily, is the only way. And what is important in that? You'll find that in all aspects of life, renunciation is very important. If you do not renounce your out-breath, how can you receive fresh air with the in-breath? You will have to learn the law of renunciation. It's very important. Don't be afraid of this law, a great law that makes you cheerful, free and happy all the time.

Who is the most ancient traveler in the history of the universe? Love. Love is the most ancient traveler in the universe. Begin examining, starting from your childhood. What does a child do? A child loves nothing else but the bosom of his mother; love travels. Child likes to have colors, striking colors. Love travels; child likes to build houses on the sand. His mother loves him and he loves his mother, but if his mother destroys the sand house, she becomes his enemy; he will no longer love his mother. He loves his house that he built on the sand. Slowly the child's love travels to another avenue. The child now loves honors, degrees, praises. Love is not satisfied, goes to another avenue and is attracted towards the opposite sex. They decide to be together, they make experiments, nothing happens. Finally the love stands all alone: I have known to love everyone but I have not known to love myself. I am a seeker; I am the fountainhead of love and light myself.

So the day we understand the law of karma and know that nothing is possible without doing our duty, then we also learn the law of giving and we learn that after giving comes freedom. Let us do our duties, but let us learn to give the fruits of our actions because otherwise, those fruits will inspire us to do more actions, and there is no end. And we can never come out of that. This is only about Vaishvanara which is only one pada. Pada means foot, but it's not like the four feet of a cow because the four feet are different. It is, rather, like the four quarters of a dollar. When you say quarter of a dollar, that quarter is not different from the dollar, it's a part of it.

To live in the external world is very important. We cannot escape it. But we have to find out the way of living happily, and there's only one way, and this is a sort of prayer. Selfless service is essential to rid one of the bondage of karma. We should learn that this is a prayer we perform in Vaishvanara, in the external world. This external world will not allow us to move on to another sphere, another level of life; will not allow us to understand various levels of life in order to attain our goal. Many of us suffer because we do not understand the importance of selfless service. Selfless service is done not for charity, because the word 'charity' is often used for gaining rewards like name and fame in this world, or for benefits in the next world. Selfless service is done because that is the only way to be free from the bondages we create through our karma. It's a great prayer, it's a great meditation, meditation in action, and that's the only way. The more you become selfless, the more you come closer to another level of life. Such a human being should learn to live for selfless service because one cannot live without doing actions, and the only way to get freedom from the bondage of your karma is to perform selfless action.

Nonattachment means pure love. Nonattachment means love without an object. There is something wrong with your love. You need someone to love and need to be loved. It means your love is poor, is weak; so weak, that it leans on something always, it needs an object, a little baby, a husband, someone. You need someone, a bag of bones, some flesh and all that, to love. And you go on saying that you love this man, but he is not the same as the one I married. He looked so tender, he looked so gentle, so friendly, now everything has changed. This sort of love that flies away is not considered love; it is considered attachment. But when your love is mingled, inseparably mingled, with nonattachment, that love is considered to be a higher love. You are a householder, practicing to attain something, not a body, which you already have. You want to attain something beyond, that which controls, the One who is the governor, the real center of motivation and consciousness within you, Atman. You forget that aim, and you expand more in the external world. Your love remains limited to the flesh, and you do not go beyond the body to the center, namely Atman. That love, which does not grow, is not love. Then what is it? It is called attachment. Attachment is the mother of all miseries.

So those who have learned to organize the external world by understanding the law of karma which deals with objects of the world, know how to relate with others, know how to deal with the gross world. Then another question is posed by life. There are many, many, many definitions of life. Physics says it is a particle; no, a ray; no, a wave. Literature says it's a long sentence with many comas, semi-colons and without any period (full stop). Philosophy says no, it's something different. Philosophers say it's a book, a manuscript written by you, half of the manuscript is missing, the beginning is missing and the end is missing, only the middle portion is with you. We have many, many definitions about life. It's a tale that has been told by the unknown and the tale goes on, related by the wise and fools alike.

Systematically you have to go inwards to the source of light and life and wisdom but first you should learn to understand and arrange your external world, and that's not so easy. You have all seen that the sadhana (path) of a householder, to live in the world with wife, children and others, is tougher than the sadhana of a swami, a renunciate. Many a time you cannot do what you want to because you will have to see to the wants of your husband, of your children, of your people, of your neighbor, of your country, of your nation, of the whole of humanity. Many times you may have to sacrifice your own little wants no matter how important. Wise people learn to deal with it by using something, not renunciation, but conquest. Conquest, by understanding vairagyam, nonattachment, by understanding love.

Another name for nonattachment is love. Nonattachment does not mean indifference. If you show indifference to someone whom you love, that is not nonattachment. In love you grow, in love you do not create a whirlpool around yourself. If you are not growing then there is something wrong with your love, there is something wrong with your concept, there is something wrong with your philosophy of life.

In love you have to grow. If your growth is stunted, well, there is something wrong. So you should learn the philosophy of nonattachment. I told you that you should learn meditation in action. But you cannot learn meditation in action if your meditation is not supported by a philosophy called nonattachment, vairagyam. People talk of renunciation, but that's a different word. I renounce this and go away; don't look at it and it's far away from me. What happened to me? I still exist and this also exists. I remember that there was a table, though I am not attached to it, but I still carry the memory. This is called renunciation. When you renounce your home, wife, children, belongings, they still exist, but you create a distance. Creating a distance means, respectable distance, mentally and physically. Renunciation means sannyasa.

There is something higher than that. That is called vairagyam, nonattachment. I am using this table here. I am using it, I am assigned to use it for a particular period. I am making use of it, and after that I leave. I should not be attached to it. A father knows, from the very day that a son is born, that a day will come when either he will make the son weep or the son will make him weep. We understand this truth. When you get married, you unconsciously know that a day will come when your husband will leave you or you will leave your husband. But you don't remember this fact consciously on the day you get married. You are getting married, you know it. No one guarantees, that you will both go together. Of course there is a method, a yoga for dropping the body together. And some of the advanced yogis, grhasthas, householders, practice that. Both husband and wife sit down together and hand over all their duties to their children, say good bye to them finally, and drop their bodies. Dropping the body means consciously changing the garment that is called body. That does not happen, if one does not know how to practice nonattachment.

The Yoga Sutras say 'no gifts.' If somebody gives you something, you definitely say, "Yes, give it to me, thank you very much. I like this gift." It means you are ayogi, that is, not a yogi. And yet yoga science says, don't take gifts from anybody. But you have only learned to ask for things. You want to have something, and when someone gives something you feel delight. Why don't you experiment in your life, at home, not with outsiders? You cannot identify yourself with an outsider. At home, learn to give. Do it two, three or four times as an experiment. Do something for your wife without her asking. Do something for your children without their asking you. This way you'll be expanding your consciousness. Find out what they need and just give it to them. Learn this habit. What will happen? Instead of being a beggar, needing something, and feeling delight when somebody gives you something, you improve and you learn to give. And that makes you generous; that gives you freedom from the bondage you have been constantly creating, consciously and unconsciously. That is the only way of dealing with the law of karma. There is no other way. The ancients said, no, there is no other way. O human being, you cannot live without doing actions. There is only one way to be free from the bondage of karma. And that freedom will come when you learn to give. Give to your people whom you consider as yours, towards whom you have assumed duties. Learn to do it with your family members. When you are selfless, then what happens to you? You don't expect from others, you just watch your actions. You see that you are being selfless. That will give you personal freedom, that will purify the way of the soul, that will help you in unfolding yourself. There is no other way for having freedom from the bondage of karma. O man, do your duties selflessly, lovingly, skillfully, effectively, freely and happily, and give all the fruits that you can to the members of your family towards whom you have to give. And experience delight.

This type of experiment was conducted by the great seers of the past, in all great traditions. Look at how all great traditions understand life, the philosophy that we should have a family, a home, where a wife learns to do actions for her husband, and the husband learns to do actions for his wife, and they both learn to do actions for their children. This way that family unit is exemplary, and from it love radiates to other neighbors. This experiment has been very, very successful because after completing this experiment, there is no other experiment. Human being could not think of any other way. There was no other way a human being could think of for getting freedom from the law of karma. If the whole universe becomes a family, and we start doing the same experiment, doing duties towards others, we will all be free human beings. We are not, because this conclusion that there should be a family and it should be an experimental ground has not been a practical success. As a conclusion, it is successful because there is no other way. But practically it is not successful. There is so much discontent, so much frustration, so much anger.

Actually, it's a sadhana (practice). Just as someone renounces his home, goes to a retreat, goes to the mountains, goes somewhere, this is a sadhana. You have to deal with your anger all the time, you have to deal with your wishes and desires all the time, and you have to deal with your wants all the time. Therefore, every home is a temple, a synagogue, a church, and every human being is a shrine. There should not be any frustration. It's a sadhana. We have to do this sadhana, there is no other way for us. So the ancients came to the conclusion that there should be family life, that there should be a home, and that all the members of that home should learn to work for each other without any reservation. Then, that concept of home and family, should expand to include the universe. "Let the whole universe become one family," was the cry of the Upanishadic seers.

Vasudaiva kutambakam, the whole universe is one family, and we are the members of that family. Let us work for each other exactly the way a family member works for other members of the family. We have not yet completed the first step, first pada. We have to make family life so successful that the idea, that ideal, expands to include the universe. Then we will all be jivan muktas. Every human being will be a mukta, a liberated being. We do not have to go for liberation to a mountain retreat, to a temple, to a swami, to a yogi; we will all be swamis, we will all be yogis.

But this experiment, being conducted for so many years, is not completely successful because we are all still individuals. The country where there is a tradition of forming teams is Japan. Japan is a small country but the Japanese are very successful. Why? I lived in Japan for many years, as many of you know. You talk to a Japanese for half an hour, and you will think that perhaps this gentleman is listening while I have been explaining my ideas. Finally, you will know that he has not heard anything. You hear, "Ho, ho, ho, ho," and that's it; because they are taught to follow their leader. They can only work as a team. When I came to America, I realized that here, there is nothing like team work. Every individual wants to understand before he does something. That's a good thing. But in the process of understanding, he doesn't form part of a team. These are experiments being conducted in various parts of the world.

See the family in which diverse ways, diverse thoughts and diverse feelings, are put together. You have seen the picture of diversity. In India there was a tradition of using symbols to interpret life on all levels. What should a good family, an ideal family, be? How should the head of the family live? At that time, most ancient time, some ten or twenty thousand years ago, we did not have any printing presses. The ancients wanted to leave some instructive and educational symbols for their next generation, for the generations to come. So they drew many, many symbols, many diverse things in one family. Have you seen Shiva? Have you heard of Shiva's family? Shiva was never born, so he never had a family. He never died, because he was never born. When he was never born, he never had a wife. Shiva here means the most ancient one, the one who established the family system, the one who wanted to give to future generations the ideal of how a family should live. Now, Shiva is always shown with a cobra around his neck. Who's going to get married to a man with a cobra around his neck? Nobody! No woman will go near him. Shiva's vehicle is a bull. Parvati, his consort, has a tiger with her all the time, as her vehicle, and their son Ganesha has a small mouse. And they live very peacefully as a family! Tiger living with a bull, snake living with a mouse, and without any disturbance! That family was considered to be an ideal family. This is called unity in diversity. This is the symbol the ancients left for their future generations.

Now, let us look at each family member, one by one. Their son Ganesha is considered to be the first one. If you want to do something you will have to worship Ganesha first, because he is highly skilled. For being successful in the world you will have to be like Ganesha. How does Ganesha look? He's the elephant god, with the head of an elephant on a human body. It's a symbol. No such human being was ever born on this earth. It's a symbol. They left it for future generations. Why the head of an elephant? Why not the head of a tiger? The elephant is vegetarian by nature. It's not violent. It only knows how to defend itself. If you are trying to be rough with an elephant, no matter who you are, tiger or any other animal, the elephant will throw you away. But only if the elephant is attacked. Otherwise, the elephant is very calm and quiet. So the leader of a family should be well skilled, well balanced so that he is calm and quiet and not at all violent. That is the significance of this symbol. Ganesha wears a thread with three strands. In all three states—waking, dreaming, and sleeping—he is fully aware of his duty towards his family. Have you seen the Chinese Buddha? Ganesha's tummy is bigger than that. Why? The head of a family will receive many suggestions every day, from morning till evening. Wife says something, son says something, daughter says something, neighbors say something, and relatives say something else. He should be able to digest all these suggestions.

Now you would like to have as your vehicle a motorbike, or a car, or maybe a small plane. Ganesha selected a mouse. Why a mouse? If by chance, the head of the family gets entangled in the network of family life, Ganesha's mouse will cut the threads and make him free. This is symbolic. If properly interpreted, these symbols will teach us how our ancients lived. From the very beginning the ancients knew that future generations, generations of human beings yet to come, will have to face this problem of diversity in life. So they created the symbols of the father with a cobra around his neck, with a bull as his vehicle, the wife having a tiger as her vehicle and the son having a mouse, yet the family living together in great harmony. This foretells the diversity of human family life. You are torn because of your thinking, because of your emotions, because of your desires. You have to work hard to establish harmony all the time and only then can you act. And if you do not do that, then you suffer. Have you not seen one with powerfully built muscles but a coward from within? Another is physically very weak but strong from within. Yet another is physically strong, but he has no love for others. We have to learn to develop ourselves from all sides, harmoniously. So let us find a formula for functioning successfully in the world. And let us start making experiments, once, twice, thrice. And when you have done these experiments successfully, apply the knowledge gained. You will find yourself successful and very happy. So far you have found delight in taking. If somebody gives you something, you smile and say, "Thank you." Now, experience the joy of giving!

There is one ananda, joy, for all of you. Your parents and grandparents have realized it, and that is called vishayananda, sensual enjoyment derived from an object. When your senses go out to an object, for example, a flower, the sensual enjoyment derived from that flower is called vishayananda. Sexual joy is considered to be the highest of all joys in the world. Why is that? When a man and woman come together, that joy cannot be retained for a long time. So you are trying to repeat the same experience again and again but that joy never lasts for a long time, there is no expansion in that joy. Finally it leads to disgust. But, by then, you become ensnared by the objects of the world, because by that time you have children, you have concerns, you have family responsibilities. You spend your whole life trying to expand that joy but nothing happens. You used to think, "Oh if I get married to this boy, or this girl, perhaps I will be in joy all the time." That's how all girls remain fantasizing in dreamland but finally they get disgusted. Look at this horrible man! I wanted him to be the man of my life, but he's horrible. By that time, it's too late. Know this fact that on this platform of the external world, called the waking state, joy is very limited and fleeting. But that taste encourages you to attain a higher joy. But where is that higher joy? You go to the sun, moon and stars and you experience all the things of the external world. If I have a bigger house, many cars, perhaps I will get that joy. You get four Bs: bank balance, bungalow, beautiful bride, baby, but nothing happens.

So you have examined the external world, the waking state you have examined; joy is there but very little and it does not last for a long time, it is called momentary joy. Now one person is not complete, so two persons unite, and think, "Let us together discover that state which is the state of highest joy." So they become like two wheels of the same chariot called life, and they both start leading their chariot forward, in search of that permanent joy, supreme joy, paramananda. It's only imagination; it is not possible to get that everlasting joy in the unity of man and woman. Perhaps if there is a God, and if I meet Him, the joy will be paramananda, everlasting joy. So they both quietly discuss, "Hey, is this life?" They laugh, "Did you get anything?" She says, "No. Be truthful, did you get anything old man?" He says, "No."

Is the consciousness that we have in the waking state under our conscious control? All the power that we have at our disposal during the waking state, is that under our control? No. Our entire universe uses adjectives like good and bad, because of only one state that is called the waking state. During the waking state of mind, you educate yourself, acquire culture. That's a small part of the totality of mind, a small part of the totality that is you. Christ knew the technique, but his guru, John the Baptist, did not. You can know something which your guru does not know.

How did Christ come in touch with that power, by which he knew more about his mind and potentials? That's why he could change water into wine. All these so-called miracles are miracles as long as you do not know them. The moment you know them, they are no longer miracles. The more you dive deep into the ocean within, the more you come out with the pearls that are lying at the bottom of the ocean.

When consciousness is turned to the external world, it is called Vaishvanara, the waking state. Now, we human beings have not yet understood the right utilization of that limited aspect of mind, the conscious mind, which is used in the waking state. Our education is trying to cultivate that part of mind which functions during the waking state, that which is conditioned by past, present and future, that which does not know what now is, does not know what now means, does not know how to attain now, how to be in now, how to live in now. We can spell the word now, but we do not know what it is. That portion of mind used in the dream and sleep states is not known to us. These states of consciousness are also not known to us. Is there any university which teaches you how to dream? You don't join a university called Dream University. So your learning and your intelligence are limited to only one aspect of the totality of the learning process. As there is a waking reality, so there is a dreaming reality. Let us first find out how the conscious mind, a small part of the totality of mind, is being trained by our educational system. This has been going on for ages, but human beings are still very crude, very primitive. The human being is called a walking animal, talking animal, because we do not know how to use the potentials that we have. Only a small part of mind, the conscious mind, is educated and then we get many degrees and designations. In the waking state, the senses contact the external world with the help of the conscious mind, and the conscious mind derives its energy from the center of consciousness. None of this is under our conscious control. From childhood, we are exposed to so many teachings, so many methods of education, so many colleges and universities. Mother says be good, be nice, be kind, be gentle. Go to church, the priest says be this, be this, be this. In school, the teacher says be this, be this. All these methods are imposed on us, yet we do not know how to utilize that small part of mind, that small amount of power, consciousness and energy, that is at our disposal.

We know so very little about ourselves. How small we feel when we realize that we only understand a little bit about the waking state, and we hardly know anything about the dreaming and sleep states, and about Turiya, the fourth state. How much do we know about our self? Look at this poverty. We know very little about ourselves. We like to hurt others because we are brutes; we do not know ourselves. That's why we do not understand that there is only one truth everywhere. Then you will not consciously hurt others, harm others, injure others, and kill others. Don't you see in your own personality that sometimes you are very cruel? A human being can be bitter, as bitter, nay more bitter, than an animal. Sometimes you are very loving, you become like an angel, and sometimes you are very indifferent. There are three states we go through each day. Actually there is only one experiencer. The waking state is not experienced by the human mind. There is only one experiencer and that is called the individual soul. When the individual soul experiences the waking state, experiences the gross world of external objects, it is called Vaishvanara or virat.

God has not created the universe. This is our thinking that God has created the universe. This is He, all this is Om. So God has never created anything. If you say God has created the universe, this is a layman's version, this is not philosophical language, and this is not scientific language. This is the language of religionists, those who do not believe in arguing logically, who do not believe in applying logic, who do not believe in purifying the way of the soul, who do not believe in any sadhana, who do not believe in any meditation. They just have faith, so they speak in such a language. Now, I want to create something. For creating something, I need some matter. So I exist and matter exists. From where has that matter come into being? Who has created that matter? So there should be another, a third existence. It's not possible for two existences to live together. There can be only one existence. So, to say that God has created the world is not scientific. The correct statement is that all this is a manifestation of the Lord. Now, there is One, only One Absolute, everywhere. Now I ask, "Is it creation of one or manifestation of one? Take the number 15. It is 15 times 1, that is, you keeping adding 1, 15 times. If you take away 1 from 15 it degenerates, it doesn't exist, it becomes 14. So there is only one everywhere, no matter where you go; there is only one self existent reality. That self existent reality was never born, never dies, is always present; so there is nothing like creation. We can call it manifestation. God has manifested this world. This gross world is called vishwa or Vaishvanara. After examining the external world, we come to know that it is definitely a reality, but not an absolute reality because this reality is subject to change. That which is ever changing cannot be considered to be absolute reality. That which goes through change, death and decomposition is also not considered to be absolute reality. Of course it is reality, apparent reality, but not absolute reality. But when we dive deep and try to examine all the facts of life in the external world, we realize that the way they look are not the way they truly are. They go on changing. This ever changing reality, apparent reality, is called vishwa.

Have you heard about the Buddha? There was a notorious bandit who used to prey on passersby. Somebody told him, "If you cut the fingers of living human beings, and collect 1001 fingers, you'll become a great enlightened one." He collected many but needed a few more. He couldn't find anybody else except his mother. So he wanted to cut his mother's finger but she tried to run away. By chance the Buddha was coming from the other side. When he saw her trying to escape, he shielded her behind him and he offered his own fingers to the bandit. When the bandit raised his sword, he could not bring it down. The sword wouldn't come down, because the Buddha believed in perfect ahimsa, non-killing, non-harming, non-injuring, non-hurting. When you learn to love everyone and practice it by non-killing, non-harming, non-hurting and non-injuring, it is called love in practice. Many of you claim to love each other, but you don't practice, those claims are mere claims. Do you think that leaning on somebody, expecting something from somebody because that somebody is your friend or your wife, is love? No! Love should be practiced in daily life. You can never think of injuring, hurting, harming or killing those you love. That's a true expression of love. It's not a mere claim without conviction.

In Sanskrit, *karana karya svabhava*, means, "The effect tells you what the cause is." Cause creates effect as a father produces a son, the son does not produce the father. So when you learn to practice in daily life these principles, these conclusions, these helpful convictions, then you enjoy them. You cannot hurt someone and say I love you. Then that love has turned into something different.

I once saw a patient in a Kansas state hospital who killed her husband because she used to love him very much. That was her story. So when I went to the hospital as an observer, she asked me, "Do you love me?" I said, "Yes." "Then why don't you kill me?" she asked. These interpretations are because of a disturbed mind. In love, you give without any condition; you don't expect anything in return. If you expect anything in return, then love is reduced fifty percent. When we talk about God, we are talking about ultimate truth. It's not like the love you express towards a human being. Love for a human being is entirely different from love for God. If two people love the same girl, they may kill each other. But if two people love God, they will love each other, for that love is universal. Love for another human being is personal. This personal love is also valid, because it teaches you how to love and expand yourself to universal consciousness.

Can I learn to understand all the states in a profound way, without any mistakes? Immediately, you will wonder, am I capable of doing this? Of course! Have I got the resources for doing this? Of course! You always think, "I am such a bad person. I am this or that." Nobody is bad and nobody is good. You are a human being; you have all the resources; you are capable; you are able, provided you know how to use your resources, how to use your inner potentials. It depends on how strong your desire is to know yourself on all levels. Do you want to know all about yourself? So far, whatever you have known, you have known from others. The Upanishads say, "Have direct knowledge." But what do you do? You are what you are because of what you have been told by your father, your mother, your friends, your relatives, your society, your schools, your colleges, your husband or your wife. Husband says you are good, you enjoy that. If someone says you are bad, you feel sad. What a philosophy you have! This way, the world will not allow you to live. Someone says you are very good; you get puffed up with pride. Someone says you are bad, you just collapse.

Never forget the great teachings of the Buddha in practical life. If you really want to survive tough times and still enjoy life, then learn from this story. Once the Buddha, as was his usual routine, went with his disciple Ananda, to beg for alms. In those days, in that small city of Rajgiri, which exists even today, the householders were disturbed because there were too many monks, too many renunciates, all over their city. There were only a few householders. One after another, the monks would come begging for alms and it was difficult for such a small village to maintain so many monks. The Buddha came to the door of one of the houses with his disciple Ananda and said, *"Bhavati bhikshan dehi."* "Give me something to eat, mother." The lady was very much disturbed. There was so little cooked food, and these monks kept coming to her door, one after another. Very disturbed, she said, "From morning till evening, I have been giving alms to these useless fellows; they are a burden to society, burden to the nation, burden to themselves. And they keep pouring in; they keep coming and going, without any consideration. They should have consideration for us." She picked up her child's filth and said, "Here, take this." The Buddha smiled, withdrew his bowl, but was not disturbed. Who was disturbed? Ananda, his disciple. Why? Because he could not tolerate this insult to his lord Buddha, the Enlightened One. He said, "Woman, I will kill you." And Buddha said, "Don't talk like that Ananda. If someone wants to give us something, please don't take it if you don't like it. If someone says you are a bad person, why do you accept it? Because you are weak. You are in the habit of accepting anything anybody gives you. You are a beggar. I want you to be a lord; I don't want you to be a beggar. You are the follower of a lord, you are a disciple of Lord Buddha, you are not the disciple of a beggar. Don't accept what others say."

Then how will you learn about yourself? You should know about yourself by your own self. Learn to understand that. We have learned that which we should not, that is, to accept anything others say. "Oh you are so great." You become very happy. You know you are not great. In your heart, you know it only too well. Yet you are happy! What is this? Hypocrisy. People are praising you for nothing and you are becoming happy. That happiness does not last for a long time because it is forced by others.

So Buddha said, "Sit down Ananda, I am going to tell you something." He took him to the peak of vultures, that's called Girhikichori, he took him there. He said, "Sit down here. I am going to tell you the secret of life. The secret of life is that if somebody wants to give you something, and if you don't want it, don't accept it. Accept only that which you want. Your want should be followed by the desire to attain your goal. Otherwise want and need are two different things. You need something, but you want something different. You are not satisfied with your needs. May you not be tossed by your wants, may you understand the importance of needs. Let your night not be laden by your desires, let your day not be laden by your wants." Thus, the Buddha taught his disciple Ananda. Don't take what you don't need. Take only that which is helpful for you on your path. He then said, "Sit down quietly. If somebody says you are great, does it affect you? It should not. If somebody says you are a very bad person, does it affect you? It should not."

This should be how you deal with the external world. There is something more you have to deal with. You can be an obstinate bull and say, "Whatever people say is not good, I don't care." You can do that. But that's also not healthy. After that comes the second phase, to sit down and introspect, "What is bad? Is it bad for me?" You can always say if it is bad for me, then definitely it should be bad for others. You are the judge. Within you there is something which is not mind, which is not intellect, which is not buddhi. That is called conscience, inner voice of conscience. Your conscience tells you. Conscience means your whole being immediately tells you. Sometimes, even though your conscience warns you, you still continue doing what you should not. It means you lack practice. You should start practicing. But in no way should you allow any complex within to hurt you, to cripple your internal strength and create barriers on the path. May you all determine that you'll complete the journey within this lifetime. You have a worldly schedule, "I will learn this much, I will work for so many years in the external world," and so on. Do you have a spiritual schedule? No. Why not? You should have one. Why do you want to work in the external world? In order to be happy. Where is that happiness? It's within. So you should have a schedule, it's not difficult, that's what the sages say. They inspire us with hope. They have attained something in their lives. They were born here on earth, they walked on the earth, they attained on the earth. And let me assure you, it's a myth that you have to renounce your home and duties to attain God. It's not necessary to do that. If you can make your spiritual schedule then it's not that difficult.

Why do you have so much stress? In modern times, this disease is spreading all over the world. This has crippled human potential; this is one of the greatest diseases among all diseases. Why? Because you are doing something which you do not want to do. You are forced to do something. You take up a job in order to pay the bills. You are living with your husband because you cannot do anything else; living with your wife because you cannot get a good wife again; living with a particular friend because a known devil is better than an unknown devil. Everywhere, people are doing that which they do not want to do, and that is giving them stress, because there is a constant inner conflict and that comes out as stress. Do not do what you really do not want to do; because if you do, later on you will repent. And if you cannot repent, that will create a sort of dis-ease which will lead to disease.

One who does not have a sense of humor is like a robot. Providence has gifted human beings with something great and that is called, how to smile. And humor is a part of a perennial smile; one should learn that. One should use humor in a pleasant way, not at the cost of others. Humor is a good quality. Socrates had that great humor. You want to know something? His wife wanted attention all the time, and that great man was a philosopher! So when he was philosophizing, she wanted to speak to him but he was always deep in his own thoughts. So she got angry and poured a bucketful of water over his head, which men deserve sometimes when they are irresponsible.

Am I wrong? So when this happened, Socrates, instead of getting angry, said, "It's not true, it's not true." His wife demanded, "What is not true?" He replied, "So far I have heard that thundering clouds do not produce rain, but that's not true! They do. You are like a thundering cloud, and see, it rained. What they say is not true, not true." Humor is something great. Many men do not understand that, and they do not utilize humor and that is why their marital life is not successful. It's good to be humorous; it's not teasing. Humor is something different, it's a great gift, if you cultivate it; it will help you.

I'll tell you a small story. There was a swami like me, who used to teach students like you. A newcomer happened to come by and started listening to the swami who was talking about nonattachment and renunciation. He explained how nonattachment means pure love, how practice of renunciation, without nonattachment, has no meaning. The passerby understood, he left, he renounced the world, he became perfect. So one day he thought, "I have attained perfection; let me go and see my brothers and sisters, perhaps they too are enlightened by this time." He came back, only to find the same swami, still giving the same discourse, to the same students, who were still sleeping!

Wise people take advantage of the right moment. Such moments come in everyone's life; they are called lucky moments. Is there anyone who has never had any supernatural experience? Everyone has, at some time or another. You have extrasensory perception. Just examine, cast your thoughts back. Look back, and you'll find that there are many things which cannot be explained. Do you think that physics is able to solve all the questions you pose?

When I left India to go to Japan, I had only eight dollars, because my government would release only eight dollars. So I went from Calcutta to Hong Kong by Cathay Pacific Airways. In the airport lounge at Hong Kong, I had a cup of tea. I paid two dollars for the tea and gave a tip of another two dollars to the waitress. Now I was left with four dollars. With four dollars I went to Japan and I was smiling. Why did I smile? People thought that this person is very happy; no, no, that's not true. I smiled thinking what a fool I am to go to Japan with only four dollars. But my master told me, "Wherever you go, you will find your friend, don't worry, your mission is with you."

There was no delay in going through customs because I did not have many belongings, only one shoulder bag. The customs official jokingly asked, "Lord, which country do you come from?" I said, "Of course from the Himalayas, India." He wanted to stop and talk to me. He said, "What is in your bag?" I said, "Garment like this, do you want to have one?" He said, "No." By chance I had kept an apple in my bag, and as you know fruits are not allowed into another country. He said, "Sir, fruits are not allowed." I said, "You can have it." He of course did not eat it, but threw it away.

I met somebody outside customs, who asked me, "Swami, where will you stay?" It was winter and I was wearing only a silken garment, and it was very cold. But I was walking like a lord, because if you have nothing, you have everything. If you don't have anyone, then definitely you have only One who is the Supreme. But you should have nothing, absolutely nothing, no support. The day I feel that I don't have any friend, then my meditation is the best. But the day I think I have somebody, that is distracting. So I was walking without a care, as I had nothing to lose. That had become my habit.

This man was very curious; he said, "May I know where you are going to stay?" There was no place for me to stay. But I suddenly remembered my master. I said, "Of course I will stay with a friend of mine." He said, "Where is your friend?" And I wouldn't say anything because I did not have any friend. The third time he asked me, I said, "I think you are my friend." And he said, "Yes I am your friend. Let's go." I followed him. We sat in his car, a big limousine with a TV and many gadgets in it. I thought this man was very poor, but when I saw his car, I realized that he was very wealthy. In broken English he told me, "I have only one son and he is dying; you should heal him; you are healer." I said, "I am not. Drop me right here." If I could not heal, that would not be good. But, suddenly, I got that tingling sensation, which indicated that my master was contacting me. I was taught to recognize that sensation. My master asked me to go ahead. So every day I used to ask myself, "What will happen to me if this boy dies?" I was afraid that the tingling sensation was wrong. This fear was in my mind, but I used to do my work. Medically, they said the child had developed hepatitis. The liver was damaged by cirrhosis. He was given no more than 3 months to live. And I started cooking for him; we used to cook meals in the Indian way. I used to feed him, I used to talk to him, I used to put him on my breast, and he became mine, very close to me. By chance, I don't know what happened, he got well and recovered completely. He is now 29 years of age, married, has 2 kids, and calls me Papa. The boy's mother came towards me, in her Japanese kimono, with a bowl of water, and both husband and wife said, "Half of our wealth belongs to you and the other half to our son. Now we will be your servants." I said, "Look here, if you give me anything he will die, so chose carefully. If I stay here, I cannot explore anything in the world." He was afraid and agreed to let me go.

So a human being becomes a sadhaka, an aspirant, when he becomes aware of many levels, starts questioning life, starts learning to examine all aspects of life, waking, dreaming, and sleeping. Who am I who wakes up, who is the experiencer of all these three states? There should be some experiencer. You say, "I dreamt, I slept, I woke up." Who is that I who experiences all this, who remains fully awake when you are in deep sleep, when you dream and when you are fully awake? There is someone beyond these three levels, or states, who remains fully awake, who does not go to sleep. And what sleeps? Does consciousness sleep, or does Atman, the individual soul sleep? Who sleeps? What happens to the memory, whose memory is it? When you start questioning all these, there is delight; someone transports you, your own questions transport you to a delightful world, questioning yourself with these amazing questions.

Analyze first the external world, that which is called Vaishvanara. What is the nature of the external world? When the consciousness rolls down, it does not come down bit by bit. It flows. When it has come out to the external world, what does it look like? If there is no consciousness, how will we know? We know, and know that we know, because of the consciousness within us. External lights, external health, is just a support. Actually we know, because the knowledge that lies within us, that helps us to realize ourselves, is already within us. But what to do? Our traditions are shallow, have nothing to do with the truth. Our cultures are sensual and do not understand this. Look, ye human being, you have not known yourself and you are trying to know others, how is it possible? The prime duty of a human being is to know himself first; and then the Self of all. The same Self that dwells within you, dwells in others. You have to know that Self, that which is called the center of consciousness. Do you think that you are able to see through your eyes? It's true that the eyes do not see. You see. The eyes are only gates, the light is within you. The senses function because there is a power within you. The moment you come to know that power, you will understand that the same power is universal power. That power operating in the external world is called Vaishvanara. The same power is called Taijasa in the dreaming state; the same power is called Prajna in deep sleep and that same power shines in Turiya.

ॐ

Chapter 4

The Dream State, Taijasa

Mantra 4

स्वप्नस्थानोऽन्तःप्रज्ञः सप्ताङ्ग
एकोनविंशतिमुखः प्रविविक्तभुक्
तैजसो द्वितीयः पादः ॥ ४ ॥

*Svapna-sthano'ntah-prajnah saptanga eko-
navimshati mukhah pra-vivikta- bhuk taijaso
dvitiyah padah*

Svapna-sthano ... taijaso dvitiyah padah
**The dreaming state, Taijasa, is the second
aspect.**

*antah-prajnah saptanga ekonavimshati mukhah
pra-vivikta bhuk*
**Consciousness is turned inward and ex-
periences subtle mental inpressions through seven
instruments and nineteen channels.**

Now, the fourth mantra says, the second aspect
is the dreaming state, Taijasa. In this state con-

sciousness is turned inward. In the dreaming state you do not deal with objects but you deal with mental impressions. These impressions are also valid because they truly represent some objects outside you. So there is a close relationship between the dreaming state and the waking state. The seven instruments and nineteen channels are the same ones as in the waking state because, in dreaming, the mind creates the same objects of enjoyment as in the waking state.

This Upanishad is leading you from the external world to the internal world, from gross to subtle. When we understand and compare this gross world of the waking state, Vaisvanara, with Taijasa, it will become more interesting. Do you think that dreams are not true? Then what is true? This waking state is also not true. Every day, you sleep and dream. Why do you ignore that reality? Why are the dreaming and sleep states less real than the waking state? When you try to compare the dreaming reality with the so-called reality of the waking state you will realize that the waking state is also a dream; maybe a dream that lasts a little bit longer than the dreams we experience when we go to sleep.

In the previous chapter, you have learnt how to deal and cope with the human helplessness that is called action in the external world without which there is no progress. Without skilful, selfless and loving action, there will be barriers, there will be bondage, and without freedom you will not be able to attain the next step. Now, let us analyze the significance of dreams. Why do we dream? Is it necessary for us to dream? How does the waking state compare with the state of dream? Do dreams comfort us, are they therapeutic? How do we express ourselves in dreams? What is that which is called deep, dreamless sleep? I think that for knowing reality we should dream, so that we may appreciate that the waking state is an even bigger dream. The subject of dreams is a very interesting subject. It does not lead you to the external world; it is leading you to the subtler, internal world.

Perhaps we will understand this external world, Vaishvanara, better by understanding the dreaming state, the state of deep, dreamless sleep and by understanding and attaining that summit which is called Turiya. With the help of Om you can do this, provided you know the technique of using Om. When you can make Om your bow, your individual soul, Atman, an arrow, and with all your might, you send that arrow to the target called Brahman, the Absolute Reality, then you will know what Reality is.

The space that is within the glass is not the horizon, but when we break the glass, the inner space merges with the outer space and becomes that. So the great teachers say, "O human being, examine all these states systematically." What is Taijasa? You think that your dreaming state has nothing to do with your life? That's not true.

If you know the method of turning your consciousness inward, you can dream during the waking state and that is called day dream. You may have seen many people coming in touch with all these natural hidden potentials of the human being accidentally. Paul, who was formerly known as Saul, came in touch with that higher potential within himself, on the road to Damascus, and then became St. Paul. Sometimes you come in touch with that potential that completely changes you, completely transforms your whole personality. And it happens when you are on the path. Why did Saul start going towards Damascus? Why not towards a hill? He could not find satisfaction in what he was doing. So when he searched everywhere, he finally set out on the road to Damascus. And on the way, self-realization dawned. Self-realization dawns when you are fully prepared. Preparation is very important in life. If you are not prepared, self-realization will not dawn. You have to prepare yourself. A human being needs to prepare himself, by understanding the instruments he has, the channels of energy he has, the resources he has.

Now he wants to search for another dimension of life by understanding the nature of the objects of the external world. I want to tell you that anything that you cannot do successfully in the external world, you can successfully do in the dream state. And as far as that dreaming reality is concerned, it's true that there is a dreaming reality. But that dream lasts for a short time compared to the longer waking dream, which is also a dream. Do you think that the duration of time makes something real? No. If you go on dreaming the same dream for 24 days, 50 days, 2 years, will it become real? Therefore, this waking state is not considered to be real as far as Absolute Reality is concerned. As this external reality is considered to be apparent reality, dreaming reality is also momentary.

So far we have examined the external world; now let us go within, to the subtler world. Let us examine the dimension called the dream world. The experiences there are a little bit different. Here in the external world you have objects, there you have impressions, cognitive experiences. As long as you dream, you are not the same as you were in the waking state. Suppose you are a king in the waking state, but you dream that you have become a donkey, and for four hours you dream that you are a donkey. You are in great agony, thinking, "Oh I used to be a king and now, suddenly, I have become a donkey."

Many a time you will find that you are being beaten up or whipped in your dream. That pain is genuine, but genuine in dreaming reality; no less genuine than this pain and pleasure which you are experiencing in the waking reality. In dream, the experiencer is experiencing only impressions, whereas in the waking state, the experiencer is experiencing the objects of the world. You find you are not satisfied with either level and the search continues.

Both the third and fourth mantras talk about seven instruments. You need to understand how the five elements, earth, water, fire, air and space, have made this jar which is called the body; and then in this jar of the body, there is a flow called breath, life breath. And there is something inside that is called ego, which has created a barrier between us and the Reality. Then you will come to know that a human being has all the potentials, but there is something that separates him from the Absolute Truth. This Upanishad says that the separation is not real, it's only a superimposition.

So that culture, that tradition we have lost. We have only learned how to sharpen our intellect, so that the intellect employs the senses and goes to the external, gross world, the world of objects, and collects data from the external world. That is all; we do not know anything beyond this. Physical sciences are trying to understand only this external world. Physicists say, "Why do you want to know anything about dream? It's sleep, it's a simple thing. You don't think of anything, you are not aware of anything, so why do you want to know more than this?" They do not understand what sleep is. Actually it's not the subject matter of physics. Psychologists are trying to understand the dreaming state which is called Taijasa.

So, to know these three aspects, waking, dream and deep sleep, you have to first understand the concept of Maya. Shankaracharya explains it in a different way. He calls Maya anadhi, most ancient. Ma means no, ya means that. Maya is that which does not exist in reality, but exists in apparent reality. Apparently it exists, but actually it has no existence of its own. One of the aspects of Maya is called mirage. When you are driving a car on a hot day, you see watery substance ahead. When you go there, you don't find water there. Optical illusions are part of Maya. Mirage is a part of Maya. It does not exist, yet it apparently seems to exist. This whole universe actually does not exist.

When I was living in the cave monastery of our tradition, I used to teach a scripture, my favorite scripture, called Panchadashi. It's one of the books of Vedanta. I used to teach about Maya all the time, but I myself never understood it. So I felt very sad. So one day I told my master, "Theoretically I know what Maya is, but I don't understand it. Give me a practical example." He smiled and he said, "Tomorrow morning I will tell you what Maya is." So I was very excited at the prospect. I thought, "If I know Maya, I will be free from the clutches of Maya, and then I will meet the Absolute." On the way, while returning after a bath in the Ganges, my master wrapped himself tightly around the trunk of a tree. And I said, "What is this? You are doing a funny thing today." He said, "I am not doing anything. Maya has done this to me. Will you please help me?" I was really young and strong. I tried my best to pull his leg, to try to release his hands and arms, but I was not successful. I said, "What is this? Please release your hands." He said, "I cannot, because this is Maya." I said, "Now Maya also has limbs! What do you mean by Maya?" When

I started perspiring, he said, "Are you tired of trying to release me from the bondage of Maya?" I said, "Yes." He said, "Now, I have decided to release myself from the bondage of Maya. And here I am, free."

You have to decide whether you will be in the bondage of avidya, ignorance, or will seek release. This is no one else's decision. You are the way you are, because you wanted to be this way. Nobody plans for you; this is your own planning. And this will go on till eternity, if you do not have an aim in front of you, and direct all your energies to understand.

Now, let's discuss this further. If we say that this tree does not exist, that is true. Apparently it exists, but it has no existence of its own for its existence lies in the seed. This is a great controversy, how karana comes out with karya, how cause produces effect. Which came first? Cause or the effect, karana or karya? They both live together. Tree lives inside the seed; it came out because it was already there. This whole universe has come out from nothingness. It means it is nothing. How can something come out of nothing? How can sakara, with form, come out of nirakara, the formless? It means this is also nirakara. Then why do we not see the universe as it is? Because of our sense perception. We don't see this world as it is when we start dreaming. We don't see this reality, that which you call apparent reality, as it is, when we go to deep sleep. We will never see the Absolute Reality, until we attain the fourth step. Now take off from the ground, in an aeroplane, and go up to a height. From there, you will not see things as they seem down here. It depends on how you see things, depends on the perspective. You are not seeing things as they are. You are seeing things partially. So partial truth is not considered to be the real truth because it has nothing to do with the totality of your experience.

You see the world with little windows called your eyes, with your little instruments, so the world is not seen as it really is. When you close your eyes, all things vanish. It depends on how you perceive things. Things are not the way they look because there is no totality of experience.

This external world is not Absolute Reality; this is all Atman, this is all truth, but a gross aspect of truth. Another subtler aspect of truth is the dream state. That's why we call it dreaming reality. The world of dream is a reality, but it's a subtler reality. It is little bit different from waking reality. As waking reality is not Absolute Reality, so also, dreaming reality is not Absolute Reality, it is apparent reality. Absolute Reality, means that which never changes, that which always exists, exists forever, that which is free from birth and death, that which is self-existent, that which is everywhere. We are studying that reality on all levels. All this is reality, all this is Atman, all this is Brahman, but on a gross level. Who projected this? From where has it come? It has come from the Absolute Reality. If it has come from Absolute Reality, then, it is complete. It is complete if you see that Absolute Reality in totality. When you don't see that unity in diversity, then it is not complete. Because of ignorance you don't see the One in many; but with wisdom you can see unity in diversity. It depends on what you want to see.

Now, nature makes the mind turn inward and that's called dream. See, there is some natural power in you that makes your mind turn inward and then you start dreaming. During that time your mind is not in touch with the external reality. You go to a different state of reality and that is called dreaming reality. When the consciousness turns from the external world inwards, then it starts getting into the land of dreams. There is actually nothing inside, yet you create something during the dream state. What do you create? That which you cannot create in the external world, in the world of objects, that, your mind creates without objects. There will be no bricks, yet your mind can create a home, a house.

That, which you call dream, can also be done consciously. You can do this, by not allowing your mind, through which consciousness flows, to employ the senses, and then you will start dreaming. That's why the yogis do not dream. You householders say, "Sweet dreams!" If you tell a yogi, "Sweet dreams," he will definitely kick you. He'll say, "What do you mean by sweet dreams? I am practicing a state of dreamless, deep, sleepless sleep and here you say 'Sweet dreams'!" If you learn that technique called sparsa yoga, yoga of touch, by knowing which you voluntarily withdraw the senses and do not allow your mind to flow with the senses, but instead turn it inward, then you start dreaming consciously.

Now, I will tell you about the variety of dreams. Many of you have gone through this; I also went through this. I dreamt that I was rushing towards the examination hall and was getting late. I was very sad because the examination hall was far away and yet I had to keep going. Most of you would have had the same type of dream because the problem is the same. There is similarity in dreaming too. If we all have problems in building a house, what type of dream will we see? We will dream about building a home in our dreams. Any desire that is not fulfilled in the external world seeks fulfillment in dreams.

Problems of the waking state create a heavy burden on the mind and dreaming is an outlet for that stress. Therefore, dream is therapeutic. Nature has created a therapy called dream. It's a great therapy. But who needs therapy? Only those who are sick. Yogis do not need this therapy. Dreams are therapeutic all right, but if you have consciously controlled that aspect which makes you sick, you do not need that therapy. So there is a way of going through the dreaming state without any exhaustion. In dream you do things which you cannot do in the external world, that's why you have dreams. Dream is a great pacifier, dream is a great remedy, dream is a great therapy, dream is a great solace; but the moment you decide that you want to dream this way, you'll never be able to dream. If you remember someone constantly, you will never dream of him. The moment you forget, you will start dreaming. It means there is some relationship between the dream and your conscious and unconscious minds.

When the mind turns inward and goes to the dreaming state it is no longer the conscious mind, because you don't have conscious control over this state. You can use this word 'control' only as long as you are on the level of the conscious mind. Are we utilizing the waking state in which the conscious mind functions, properly? The more we use it properly, according to our capacity, our fullest capacity, the more brilliant we become. But we are considered to be brilliant only as far as this waking state is concerned. You cannot say you are champion dreamer!

Therefore, you should understand that the waking state is not the only state that we experience; we go beyond that to experience the dreaming state. The portion of mind which is used during the waking state, conscious mind, is but a small part of the totality of mind. The dreaming mind and sleeping mind are much vaster. Science does not know how to get into the dreaming mind. Science has not created any device which helps us to dream according to our wishes. Science can help in giving you anesthesia and putting you into an artificial sleep, but that artificial sleep is useful only to relieve you, to detach you, from the pain experience, not to bestow happiness on you, not to bestow joy on you, not to make you understand something about life, it's only a pain reliever. Knowledge alone, can help; wisdom alone, can liberate. So you realize, that the portion of mind which dreams, is not under your conscious control.

So now we come to the unconscious mind. The unconscious mind has a large field. Dreaming and deep sleep are included in the field of the unconscious mind. Now, there are varieties of dreams. Don't think that if you have learned to make your mind inward, you have controlled the entire dream world. If you overeat one day, and this creates some gastric problem, that day you will dream. That is not really a dream. It is called a nightmare, because your mind, your jiva, that is experiencing the dream, is influenced by the external problem. What is a nightmare? A nightmare is a part of dream that comes from the field of the unconscious, but is not actually a dream, it is an artificial dream.

Now there are many categories of dreams, let us classify them one by one. This will help those of you who are therapists. Dream interpretation is very interesting, but often it's just like groping in the dark. What happens in darkness? In darkness if there are white cows, or cows of any color, you don't see anything; you see everything dark, only darkness. Dream interpretation can be understood by understanding the behavior of the patient first. How does the patient behave? As you behave, so do you dream. I have never seen a fanatic Mohammedan dreaming of Christ. I have never seen a staunch Christian dreaming of the Buddha. So what does dream mean? It does not reflect only the way you think or the way you behave, but reflects the way you are, your whole life pattern. For studying your whole life pattern there is only one branch of psychology, that is behaviorism.

So to understand the dream world, we will have to examine the cultural background. If you are a therapist and a patient comes to you, you will have to first find out about the patient's cultural background, because that person's dreams will be according to his cultural background. Suppose you know English and other languages as well. Which is your primary language? You cannot have many primary languages, it's not possible. Your primary language is that language in which you dream. Otherwise, when you write or speak in a different language, you are subtly translating in your mind from your primary language. You have only one language and that is the one in which you dream.

So for dream interpretation, you will have to know the cultural background of the patient, four aspects of the cultural background. All dreams are related to the four primitive fountains: food, sleep, fear and sex. Let us take the simple example of food. Suppose I am hungry, and I am a vegetarian, I will never run after a goat in my dream, to kill it, cook it and satisfy my hunger. I will instead dream of running towards a field to try to pick some potatoes, tomatoes, spinach or some other vegetable because I am a vegetarian. Even when I am very hungry, I will never chase a lamb or a goat; I will look for vegetable fields, I will look for fruit trees. Why? Because of my habit patterns, as far as eating food is concerned.

So whenever you want to interpret dreams, you should find out from the patient, what his or her favorite dishes are, what food he or she eats. Sometimes a patient says turkey; another patient says red meat, this meat, that meat. You can easily find out. One of the great yogis said that your thinking is exactly according to the food you eat.

But food is only one fountain. Sleep is another important fountain. If you have not slept for 2-3 days, or for 24 hours, you won't have time to dream; you will not dream that day. I can challenge you on this; if I don't allow you to sleep, you will not dream because, what is important for you? To dream or to sleep? Both are therapies. One works on your frustrations, unfulfilled desires; another works on your physical and mental abilities, mental necessities, your need for rest. So your consciousness postpones dream: I have to sleep now, because that's necessary for my body and mind; I can dream tomorrow or day after tomorrow. Sleep is a greater necessity, a greater therapy than dream. But dream is definitely a therapy, and needs interpretation and can be interpreted by understanding the four primitive fountains of human life. You can do it for yourself, try it.

The waking state depends on sensory perceptions; the dreaming state depends on mental conditions, deals with mental frustrations, desires which are not fulfilled in daily life; so dream is a great therapy. Dream is definitely therapeutic. If someone doesn't dream, either he's sick or he's a yogi. There is similarity, but it's not the same thing. Dreaming is therapeutic, but if you are meditator, it's a waste of time. If you are sick, if you do not know what meditation is, then it is a must. Any dream can be interpreted by understanding what type of food you eat, when you go to sleep, what is the quality of your sleep, what is your philosophy towards sex, what role do you think sex plays in your life, what is your attitude towards death, are you afraid of death, afraid of being killed in an accident. If you are afraid of an accidental death, then you will always be at risk of a fearful accident. Fear invites danger! Young girls, all over the world, have this dream of being chased by somebody, no matter which culture they come from. This is not a cultural hang up. Somebody very ugly is chasing them, an ugly man with a knife, a sword or a gun, and they are running away. Then the girl wakes up in fear, perspiring. Students dream about going to the examination hall, being late, not being able to find the place. Dream also depends on your internal schedule. What schedule do you have for yourself?

There is a fine demarcation, a transitional state, between waking and dreaming. And, in Sanskrit, that is called unmani awastha. There is another such transition between dreaming and sleep called ahladini and that between sleep and Turiya is called samadhi. So there are actually not three but seven states, if we include the transitions between the three states. We are going into greater detail.

If you just sit down and try to find out how exactly you go into the dreaming state, you'll find that these forms, worldly objects, are becoming hazy, and finally you are simply detached from these forms, from the world of objects. But inside you, the impressions of these forms are there. And you have the capacity to magnify, to reduce, to distort, to do whatever you want. Outside you don't have that capacity. In the waking state, your mind does not have the ability or capacity to create a horse out of a monkey. But in dreams, your mind has that capacity. It means you are free to do anything in your dream state, there is no law. In the external world there are laws. If you try to kill somebody, you will be arrested, you will be punished; but in a dream, if you want to kill somebody, you just go ahead. So in dreaming state you have that freedom. But what do you do? You do not understand, you do not know the technique of how to creatively use this freedom of the dream state. If you learn how to use that freedom, my Lord, you will be great! You can be the creator of this world and of many, many worlds.

If you have not seen, heard, read, or in some way come in contact with something, how can you dream of that thing? The greatest dreamers of the universe are the great ancients, great people whom we follow today, we call them avataras, we call them seers, we call them messengers; they were the greatest dreamers. But they could not dream of anything more than the average human. Take the example of an angel. That dreamer, who created an angel was a great dreamer, but what could he do? He could not go beyond the concept of a human being, a good human with a gentle human face, but with a bird's wings. He could not imagine anything more than a human with the wings of a bird. The scientist who created an aeroplane could not imagine anything more than two wings. The scientist who created a vehicle could not imagine more than four wheels. There should be some place from which the thinking process starts. Suppose I think of a watch, then I will think of the wrist. If I think of a clock, immediately, I will think of the wall. So there is also a link and process system in your dreaming. Suppose your husband or your children go somewhere far away. You love them, and they love you, but you do not receive any telephone calls or letters. Suddenly, one day you will find that you are talking to them on the phone in your dream, that's dream therapy.

There are prophetic dreams too. After all, as it is important for us to know that there is Atman, Atman also knows that there is something called the body, its temple. I tell you, any accident that happens is not an accident. You know it and you invite that situation for yourself. Swami Rama Tirtha explains it this way, fear invites danger, and any accident that occurs is by self-invitation. You do not want to meet with an accident, yet you are afraid of an accident. That fear strengthens and creates the accidental situation.

Let me tell you something. In childhood I used to play with cobras, with bear cubs, with tigers, but when I came in touch with English-speaking children in school, somehow or other I developed a phobia. I somehow created a fear of snakes in my psyche. That phobia grew stronger in my heart and mind; a time came when wherever I went, I used to check the room, pillow case, even my pockets, for snakes. A phobia is strengthened out of fear. I never examined that fear, that was an imagined fear picked up from others. Actually, there is never any fear inside, it comes from outside. We entertain it, we don't examine it, and that's why it gets strengthened. So one day, I was sitting on the bank of the Ganges, just next to my ashram. There was no barrage dam in those days, you could see the Ganges flowing by. So I was sitting, not knowing that there was a cobra curled up beneath me. So two or three times, I stood up and sat down, and the cobra would also lift up and curl itself down. It happened as a natural situation. Now, see what happened. A swami saw this and he shouted, "Be careful, there is a cobra curled beneath you." He asked me to be careful but I did not know what to do. When a parent says, "Be careful," it does not mean that it's a cause for alarm. But I got alarmed and I ran. When I ran, the cobra gave chase. Usually, a cobra never chases anyone. Why should a cobra chase somebody? You are not food for the cobra. So cobras usually don't chase human beings. It was my negative mind that was dragging the cobra along. I found out too late that it was fear that was dragging the cobra along.

There are people who dream excessively. Perhaps, there is something wrong with them. This is called artificial dreaming. Such dreams have nothing to do with the anxieties, frustrations, unfulfilled desires and all that. There is nothing to do, so I am dreaming. I want to sleep, but I am not getting sleep because I rested the whole day and I am not tired. So, I start dreaming. Daydreaming is different from artificial dreaming. Dreams which need interpretation for the sake of therapy are different. Dreams, like an ugly man chasing a girl, called nightmares, are entirely different. Dreams that students have of running towards the examination hall, are also nightmares, but of a different quality.

Prophetic dreams come when there is spontaneity. Spontaneity, here means without any anxiety, without any awareness; they just roll down from the valley of the center of consciousness and they are so clear. Such dreams often come in the early morning hours. Do you know why? Because by that time your body has taken rest; it is possible for you to dream even after deep sleep. There are two types of dreams, dreams before sleep and dreams after sleep. A dream does not know whether it should come before sleep or after sleep, it can come at both times. Such prophetic dreams come after you have had deep sleep, when you are fully rested, and your mind has no content, there are no impressions in the mind, there are no anxieties in the mind, mind is not aware of anything that can be considered mine or thine, there is no jealousy and discrimination. During such times a hunch, something, rolls down from the infinite library within and that dream is called a prophetic dream, and it comes true. It happens, sometimes, that prophetic dreams are meant to help you, to guide you, by giving you a glimpse, a pleasant glimpse, of the future. Prophetic dreams are not related to the past. They bring the future into the now and that's a great quality of such dreams. But it happens rarely and only early in the morning when you are fully rested. During that time, you are like a prophet; you are not touched by worldly problems, with the stains of a self-created philosophy of sin. You are free from these problems.

There is a different approach to interpretation of thought patterns. This conscious interpretation of the impressions which create dreams is very healthy and helpful. You can ask your patient, "What do you think about most?" "About my husband." It means there is something, either she loves her husband very much or she is afraid of him and is insecure, there is something wrong. "How do you feel when you think about him?" "Horrible." It means there is some marital problem. So just as you can interpret dreams, you can interpret these particular thought patterns.

When a thought comes, the thought expresses itself with a symbol, remember this. Sound creates a form. Thought creates sound and form both, so you will find relationship of thought, sound and form. They are very close. All the forms have come out of sounds. There cannot be a form without a sound. There cannot be any form without thought. My thought created this building, your thought created that building. This whole creation is a thought. So creation virtually means thought. When you learn to inspect within, that's called introspection. In the beginning, it may be difficult for you to start doing introspection of your thought patterns. This is because they are your thoughts, stored by you, and you get involved with them. But after sometime, when you have learnt how to introspect, thoughts will come and go away and you can inspect the thoughts without getting involved. In a way, this introspection is a type of interpretation, exactly like the dreams you interpret; it's very healthy and helpful. You wonder, "Why is this thought coming to my mind again and again?" Suddenly, you meet someone at the airport. You forget everyone, your children, your home, and you keep thinking of that person. Why is that? Why did you like that person? You can interpret all these symbols because dream is also symbolic. Sometimes you cannot interpret some of your dreams, because the symbols that you see in the dream are not known to you. But when you learn to understand your thoughts, you understand the symbols, and you also understand the sound associated with the symbol, the form. You then realize the close relationship between thought, sound, and form.

Dream interpretation is possible if you try to observe your thought patterns before you go to bed. That is considered to be introspection, inspecting within, inspecting your imageries, trying to understand what type of images are coming into your mind. You'll find that most of the images are related to those duties of yours which you could not accomplish in the daytime or which you have postponed for many days. So these impressions start coming forward for completion, for your attention. Thus, you can easily see and watch these particular symbols. There is one difference here, dream is more symbolic and you need to interpret symbols. You often see dreams symbolically. If you see a mountain in front of you all the time in your dreams, you can interpret that you have a desire to attain the highest summit, yet you are not capable of doing that. That desire has a dual nature, awareness of your inability and at the same time the desire to attain the summit. You can interpret your dreams, so that dreams are understood by the conscious mind. This way, you understand that part of your nature which is not normally understood in the waking state. Many a time you forget your dreams. You forget them because they are not that important, just as you forget many things which happen in your daily life. But important things you do not forget. So is the case with dreams. It means that there is a close relationship between actions in the external world and your dream world.

I told you a Hindu will not dream of the Prophet Mohammed fighting in the desert. A Christian will not dream of Krishna playing his flute under a tree. We all have our samskaras, subtle unconscious impressions, and these samskaras lead us in dream too. The best type of dream is prophetic dream, but prophetic dreams come only when you have done your meditation and there is nothing to disturb your dreaming state. Then, there is a space for prophetic dreams, but you cannot call out, "O prophetic dream, come to me." They come by chance, spontaneously, not voluntarily. They may come voluntarily to those who have access to that infinite library within which is called library of consciousness, library of knowledge. A part of your unconscious mind is unique. But remember that all unconscious states are not considered to be part of dream and sleep states. The state of deep sleep, according to yoga, as well as our philosophy, is a very productive state.

In the dream state, you are experiencing internal objects coming up from your mind, the impressions in the storehouse of merits and demerits that is called the unconscious mind. But in deep sleep you do not discriminate, you do not see anything, you do not feel anything, and that state is a natural gift because you are led to a state of bliss. You remain in a state of bliss.

Truth comes out during the dream state, so don't think that the dream state is not an important state. You can never hide any of your feelings during the dream state, no matter how great you are. You have no such control, unless you are a perfect yogi. Then you will not dream.

When somebody is under the influence of anesthesia, and when he starts to come out of that anesthesia, that state is also a dream-like state. During that time, I have seen police interrogating patients. A husband always pretended that he never went out with other women. And his wife thought that her husband was an angel. But suddenly, something happened and he was taken to the hospital. In the hospital, the wife became friendly with the nurse. This is a true story. The nurse told the wife, "Do you want to know the real character of your husband?" She said, "What do you mean? My husband is very honest with me." She said, "All husbands are honest. But what to do with their nature? By nature they are polygamists." The wife retorted, "But my husband is not like that." The nurse said, "I don't believe that, all men are like that. I don't trust them because they are made that way." And they started arguing. The nurse said, "If they don't go out with other women, they at least think and brood about such things, even in their dreams. Ok, your husband is now under the influence of anesthesia. When he starts coming out of anesthesia, I'll tell you and you can start putting questions." The wife agreed. She asked, "Did you have any girlfriend?" He said, "Yes." "What was the name of your girlfriend?" He said, "Leela." I know all this because this case was referred to me later on. The wife was very disturbed. She said, "I thought my husband was an angel, but my husband had a girlfriend before he married me and her name was Leela and he never told me this." I tried my best to pacify her, I could not. Even today she's prejudiced. She looks after him, adores him, does all things for him but in her mind, is the thought, "All men are like that."

The scriptures say that if you learn to meditate before you go to bed, you will definitely not have nightmares. Some children are afraid of the dark, some boys are afraid of being killed by bad men, some girls are afraid of being chased by bad men. Such nightmares occur because of hearing things, reading stories, seeing movies, and the mind distorting these inputs when it becomes weak. Whenever you are weak, you distort things. Distortion comes through weakness. A strong person will never distort things. If your eyes are 20-20, they will see things properly. But if you have some problem in your eyes, you may see things in a distorted form. Optical distortion is well known. Distortion by the mind is also well known and is like a mirage. The distortions of avidya and Maya are well known.

I am going to explain to you some techniques. It does not matter if you cannot twist your body and legs; sometimes learning such new techniques from the easterners can be painful, because you are not allowed to sit on the floor. I have seen in modern homes, if a child sits on the floor, the mother spanks the child, asking it to get up and sit on the chair. This does not allow the lower limbs to be flexible, and then one day you become a robot.

Now listen to this interesting observation. That particular thought which occupies your mind very often, is some errand that you have not finished, some work left undone. For example, for many days, you have wanted to buy a car but you have not yet been able to do so. That unfinished business will absorb your mind more when the train of images is coming. The impressions are stored in the unconscious mind, and when the body is relaxed and the conscious mind is relaxed, then the train of images comes forth. When that happens, you will notice that the mind is paying attention towards one particular image, a car, more than other images, because you think you want it badly. This is called recalling that impression consciously which is bound to give you a dream later on. This way you can get freedom from the impressions you have stored in the unconscious.

What attitude should you have during such introspection? Decide, that I will not be swayed by anything that comes into my mind during this time; I will learn to let go. You will learn to merely observe, without getting attached to the impressions already stored in your mind. You store those impressions which you love or hate. Sometimes hatred is stronger than love; your love is poor because your hatred is very strong. Those impressions are already there, so they will come forth. There are many varieties of impressions that you have. You can understand your actual inner functioning if you analyze and understand these impressions by introspection.

So the dream state is when consciousness is turned inward. But for a yogi, that inward turning is voluntary and done consciously. It's called pratyahara, withdrawal of the senses from the external world, consciously. The yogi can consciously go into the dream and sleep states. Whenever you are unconscious, know that you are touching the sleep state. A yogi does not sleep to attain the fourth state of Turiya. You have to be conscious to attain Turiya. A yogi has to control sleep for attaining this, which is why Turiya is also called sleepless sleep.

So waking state has some relationship with the dream state. All that cannot be accomplished during the waking state, you accomplish in dreams. But the yogi says no, why not sit down and meditate before going to bed? I told you it is easy for you to analyze your dreams, to interpret your dreams. Sometimes when you forget your duties, when you postpone them, when you forget engagements which are lying in the basement of your mind, dreams come up and remind you. Dreams can disturb you, dreams can make you joyous, dreams can give you a glimpse of a part of your personality, dreams are therapeutic, but yogis say, "It's all a waste of time. We don't have time to dream, why should we dream?" For that they sit down and meditate.

ॐ

Chapter 5

The State of Deep Sleep, Prajna

Mantra 5

यत्र सुप्तो न कञ्चन कामं कामयते,
न कञ्चन स्वप्नं पश्यति, तत् सुषुप्तम् ।
सुषुप्तस्थान एकीभूतः प्रज्ञानघन
एवानन्दमयो ह्यानन्दभुक् चेतोमुखः
प्राज्ञः तृतीयः पादः ॥ ५ ॥

Yatra supto na kanchana kamam kamayate na kanchana svapnam pashyati tat sushuptam. Sushupta-sthana eki-bhutah prajnana-ghana evanandamayo hy-ananda-bhuk cheto-mukhah prajnas tritiya padah.

Sushuptata-sthana ... prajnas tritiya padah
The state of deep sleep, Prajna, is the third aspect.

Yatra supto na kanchana kamam kamayate na kanchana svapnam pashyati tat sushuptam.
In this state, there is neither desire nor dream.

eki-bhutah prajnana-ghana
All experiences merge into the unity of undifferentiated consciousness.

evanandamayo hy-ananda-bhuk cheto-mukhah prajnas
The sleeper is filled with bliss, experiences bliss, and can find the way to knowledge of the preceding two states.

Now, before I tell you something about deep sleep, I want to tell you that deep sleep and death are like twin sisters. And if you understand deep sleep well, you understand death too. If you understand death well, you can easily understand deep sleep too. Suppose someone lives for one hundred years. How many years will he sleep? At least twenty-five to thirty years. If somebody sleeps thirty years, he is dead, because he is not dreaming and he is not awake. He is in deep silence. When you are not awake, when you do not dream, you go to deep sleep and if that deep sleep continues for a long time that is called death. Sleep is not terrifying. You work the whole day and finally the long awaited time for sleep comes. You look forward to falling asleep because the state of deep sleep gives you comfort.

So here the Upanishad calls it Prajna, knowledge that is enlightening. Let us understand what sleep is. Where does the great Atman, Ishwara, the inner Lord, reside? The dreaming state is called Hiranyagarbha, the golden womb. Sleep is the golden gate of light. You at least reach the gateway to enlightenment, because the next step is Turiya.

How to practice that which is called yoga nidra, yogic sleep? There are a few things that I would like you all to practice. I am talking to you on the basis of the experiments conducted by the yogis. They came to certain conclusions which I am going to put in front of you. Have you ever heard of walking sleep? It is not the same as sleep walking which is considered to be a sort of disease. In sleep walking, you walk but you are not conscious. My walking sleep was done consciously. I used to meditate for many hours, so I did not have time to sleep. Whenever I did not have time to sleep, I slept while I walked. I was doing it consciously. I started practicing it by giving my body complete rest. My mind and brain and nervous system were at complete rest, yet I remained fully conscious. I did many experiments on it and I used to record my findings. The sleep of that state is very rewarding. What rewards can you get?

Sri Harsha was one of the greatest scholars of India. He wrote a book with a very difficult name, *Khandakhandakhadyam,* a name which no layman can remember. He was insulted by the scholars of India who could not understand his writings. When you do not understand something, it's easier to just condemn it, rather than admit to lack of under-standing. Sri Harsha became sad thinking, "How stupid these scholars are, they hate me, they despise me, it's better for me to leave this place." So he left his city and went away to Kashmir, the northern part of India. One day, he was sitting by the lake. There were two women who started fighting. And they were fighting fiercely, pulling each other's hair, scratching each other's face; you can imagine how women fight. They were arrested by the police and produced in court, in front of a judge, who was the king of that state. They also brought Sri Harsha to court as he was a witness. He told the judge, "Sir, I don't know your language, but I can reproduce what one woman said and I can also reproduce what the other woman said. But I don't understand what they said." The judge was surprised, "Can you do it?" He said, "Yes." "What's your name?" "My name is Sri Harsha. I am a scholar and the author of *Khandakhandakhadyam*." So the king postponed the judgment to the next day so that he could ask the scholars of his court about Sri Harsha. They said, "If he is truly Sri Harsha, then our state is very fortunate to have him as our guest." So people came from all over the kingdom to watch him in court. He reproduced exactly all that the two women said, without knowing a single word of the Kashmiri language!

How did he do that? He knew how to get into a state of mind called dharma megha samadhi, which is just a little bit lower than perfect samadhi or kaivalya samadhi. In this state he could record and recollect everything. You may speak Hebrew, or you may speak German or French, it doesn't matter. The recording will go on and it can all be reproduced. In this state, you will not forget anything, unlike dreams, which you may forget. In this state called sleepless sleep, you can reproduce what is heard verbatim. You are in deep sleep, yet you are fully conscious. What is deep sleep? It is a state in which you are not aware of the objects of the world, you do not have any dreams, and you do not have any content in your mind. If you can learn to empty your mind completely, if you can withdraw consciousness from the sleeping state, from the dreaming state, from the waking state, then you can attain this state of sleepless sleep.

Deep sleep is a state of bliss. If you do not sleep for many days, can you enjoy anything of the world? Come on: Choose that which you consider most enjoyable. Now, can you enjoy that if you are not allowed to sleep? What do you do after you have enjoyed the best of things? You want to rest, you want to sleep, because sleep is even more enjoyable. Ultimate enjoyment for most human beings is sleep. But the yogis say that sleep is not the ultimate enjoyment. When a fool goes to sleep he wakes up as a fool, there is no change in him. There is no transformation. This is not the case with Turiya. If a fool, by chance, goes to Turiya, he will emerge as a sage. By chance, Saul came in touch with that great inner power and his whole life was transformed; he became St. Paul. Valmiki was a notorious robber who used to rob everyone, even swamis and sadhus. When he came in touch with that great power, Turiya, his whole life was completely transformed. Some sudden grief, some accident, some loss in life, may allow you to come in touch with that inner power. When you lose someone who is very dear to you, you become disillusioned with this world. You wonder, "Is this what I was expecting from the world?" You become completely detached from the whole world, because till then you had never realized the meaning of life on this worldly stage. By the time you have cried your heart out, by the time you have buried that person, you will have become like a sage. But when you return home, you think, "I have to do this, I have to do that," and you lose that detachment. If at that particular moment when you had that genuine detachment, vairagya, you had resolved to yourself, "I want to search for truth, for reality; I realize that all this is false," perhaps that moment would have led you to the highest wisdom.

Sleep can give great knowledge, Prajna, provided you understand what it is, understand its true nature. So let us systematically explore all these three dimensions and then try to go on to attain the fourth dimension called Turiya. Now, scientists do not understand death nor have they studied the anatomy of sleep in depth. This Upanishad says that the state of deep sleep is the gateway to real knowledge. It is a state witnessed by Ishwara, the inner Lord, who can see, who can watch, who can understand, the other two states of waking and dreaming. The state of deep sleep can lead one to knowledge of the higher state of Turiya, the fourth state, as well as the two lower states of waking and dream. I will explain to you how in deep sleep you are full of wisdom and how this state prepares you for Turiya, the next and ultimate step.

Scientists say you do not need to understand anything about sleep. I tell you that if you do not know anything about sleep and if you do not even try to learn about sleep, then how will you go to the fourth state, Turiya? The state of sleep is called anandamayo, permeated by bliss. In deep sleep you are in a very blissful state. It is even more effective than anaesthesia in relieving pain. When you are under the influence of anesthesia, the body is not rested. But in deep sleep, the body, the breath, the mind, everything is rested. Because there is no content in the mind, both divisions of the autonomic nervous system, sympathetic and parasympathetic, are rested. They are fully asleep. That which can be bestowed by sleep, cannot be bestowed in any other way.

There is a very close relationship between sleep and dream. You cannot go to bed without dreaming. How can you observe this? One day you should decide, let me see what happens when I go to sleep. I did it and I could not sleep for many days. I thought, "Let me see what happens, at that exact moment when one goes to sleep." I wanted to watch that moment, to see what happens to me. For eighteen days I did not sleep. My eyes were very swollen, my body became very heavy. I could not walk. I could not attend to anything because I wanted to watch what happens when sleep comes. After eighteen days, something clicked within and then I did not know what happened, I was in deep sleep. Then my master said, "No. You are watching something, but you are not fully prepared and you are not equipped for that. There is a way of doing it. And that way is called yoga nidra."

How to sleep consciously? You people sleep because it's 10:00 p.m or 11:00 p.m. or midnight. You have to go to work in the morning, so you need sleep. What is this? This is a preconceived idea. This is called hypnotic sleep. Your sleep is not natural. Your sleep is hypnotic sleep. That's not very good.

Freud, Adler, James, all used the technique of hypnosis. They used it because they understood something about sleep. Why did they stop that sort of therapy? Why is hypnosis not so popular today? Because James and Adler found out, that in hypnosis, the patient came in touch with something that created serious problems. Some of them also died during that therapy. They hypnotized patients, and at the end of the session, when they told the patients to come out, some patients would say that they did not want to come out of that state. The patient was no longer under the control of the hypnotist, and hypnosis works only as long as the patient is under the hypnotist's control. Patients did not want to come out because they felt happy in that state.

Many people have a fear, that if they go to sleep, they might not come back. Many have that phobia. They are afraid of falling asleep, so they do not get good quality of sleep. We have many such fears, many types of fears. Some are very bold, they say they are not afraid of even a tiger, they can kill a tiger with their bare hands, but the moment they see a spider, they are terror-stricken. We all have some sort of fear. A teacher has fear that his students might misunderstand him. A student has fear that he might not understand his teacher's language. This goes on all the time, we always have some sort of fear. We should learn to examine our fears. Why are we afraid? You'll find, on analysis, that expectation is the mother of all fears. I will not be afraid of you if I don't expect something from you. If I don't have a desire, if I don't have a relationship, that you are my student and I am your teacher, why should I be afraid of you? I am afraid of you because we have a relationship, with certain expectations.

So there are many types of fears we have within us. We have a body that is called fearful body, we live in that body, as long as we remain awake, as long as we dream. But when we go to deep sleep, mind has no discrimination, consciousness is not in the external world, not in the cognitive world, not in the dream world; but the consciousness is within you

One thing I can tell you. After enjoying all the joys, what do you finally do? Don't you get tired? You go to sleep. You always say, "Honey, let me sleep. Let me take rest." It means you long for rest. You go to rest. And when you wake up you find that you are not rested. So every day you are fatigued and you wait for sleep, and that sleep does not refresh you. So Swami Rama says that there is something called sleepless sleep. If you learn to meditate, that will give you greater joy. Sleep you will get every day, but that joy you will get only in meditation. The highest of all joys can be attained only through meditation. I'm telling you this. Nothing else can give you that joy.

If I'm in bliss now, I can remember it tomorrow, as you generally do. You may tell your husband, "Honey, we enjoyed life better last year, why are we fighting this year?" You remember the bliss of last year, because this year you are in conflict. When we are in deep sleep, do we enjoy the bliss consciously? No. Because, if we enjoy consciously then it is not sleep. We remember it when we are awake and we then compare it to the lack of bliss in the waking state or during dreams. Yogis say this is not a good thing. If we enjoy bliss now, we should learn to enjoy it consciously. We do not need to be awake to watch and to observe and to get confirmation that we enjoyed deep sleep. Don't forget that you do not totally sleep even when you are in deep sleep. We have done simple, crude experiments on it. I used to twist a piece of paper, and when one of my teachers was fast asleep, I would insert it into his nose, or in his ear. He would try to push it away and then go back to sleep again. A part of you remains awake even when you are in deep sleep.

Which part of you remains awake? That which does not know how to sleep, that which does not need sleep. That is your jivatma, individual self, which is always there, even today, at this very moment. But when it is experiencing the gross world, we called it the waking state, and when it starts experiencing the impressions stored in the mind, it is called the dream state. If both states are absent, there is no content in the mind, no desires no dreams. Then you experience who you are. Jiva, your individual soul experiences the joy of deep sleep. Therefore deep sleep is not an inert type of experience. Some experiments should be conducted. What is deep sleep? Why do you get joy in deep sleep? A patient cries with great pain without anesthesia and after some time, when he is tired, then he goes to sleep and he doesn't cry. He is free from pain. Is that deep sleep an inert experience, something that makes us unaware, that puts us into the lap of unconsciousness? The yogis go consciously from waking state into meditation. They close their eyes, they don't allow their senses to function, they don't want their mind to contact the external objects through the senses. They don't hear, they don't see, but they still think. The images that are stored in the unconscious mind come forward, and if they are witnessing them consciously, that's part of meditation. If they are not witnessing them, but become influenced by the impressions, then that state is called dream, not meditation. So yogis like to watch and inspect the train of mental images.

Are our mind and senses under our control in the waking state? No. And in dreams, they are definitely not under our control, but during deep sleep, the Lord of life teaches you how to have control over them. That which you cannot do during the waking state, you are able to do in deep sleep. While awake or in dreams, you do not forget that you exist, you do not forget that you are the son of so and so, you are a doctor or a psychologist, you are good, you are bad, you are the owner of this property or that property. But during sleep you completely forget, because all that is a superimposition. Had it been reality, how could you forget? Whatever you think about yourself, if it had been truth, you would not have forgotten it. Why do you forget it? Because this is not reality, truth. This is not a part of Absolute Reality. Dream may tell you that you are a great scholar. Or you may dream that you are stupid, you are a fool, you do not know anything. And you feel bad and you cry and you feel pity for yourself. But suddenly your wife comes, so you compose yourself, you stop crying. And this is all a dream.

Now you have certain habit patterns, some of which have a deep impact on your life. Throughout the day you do many things, fulfill your duties, but there may be one thing that you repeatedly think of, in the midst of all this activity. It means that this particular habit has a deep impact on your life. Such deep impressions do give you dreams again and again, dreams relating to that habit pattern. It could be anything. So in dream, you watch the imagery and when the images are exhausted, you go to that field which is called deep sleep. There you don't experience the gross world, you don't experience the images, you experience joy. In yoga nidra, yogic sleep, you try to maintain consciousness during this experience of bliss. In the beginning you will fall sleep, while practicing yoga nidra, but if you persist you can remain fully awake, yet you are in deep sleep. You are very close to the king whom you longed to see, made many efforts to see. You go before him, but you fall asleep. There is another person, who is sitting there, talking to the king, they are both very close. One who is not conversing, is in sleep, one who is conversing is in samadhi, that is the difference between samadhi and sleep.

So, in that state of samadhi, prajnata samadhi, there is still duality, but there is no third. You are talking, you are conversing, you are having a dialogue, pleasant dialogue. You are constantly thinking but there is only one thought, being directed to the center of consciousness. That is called samadhi. Still that is a lower samadhi because there are two, you exist, and there is someone called the Supreme Lord, who also exists. The highest samadhi you realize in Turiya, when you become one with the Absolute, like the river becomes one with the ocean, like a drop of water becomes one with the ocean. But these are all super-impositions. The same experiencer who is in bliss says, what happened to my dreams? Dreaming reality is illusory. Even this waking reality is illusory. Had it been a total reality, Absolute Reality, how could you dream? If dreaming reality were true, then how could you remain awake? So, both are not true. There is something higher which is true. Then you go to sleep. In deep sleep you find great joy. But you go to sleep with the expectation of awaking, of coming back.

Yogis enjoy that deep sleep consciously. They can record things better during that time. I used to practice it. I am not boasting, merely stating facts. You can connect me to a machine which will show that my brain has started creating delta waves more than seventy-five to eighty-five percent of the time. That is a clear indication that I am in deep sleep. And during that time you can tell me something. I will be recording it accurately and when I wake up, I can reproduce all that you told me, verbatim. It is a practice, a simple practice because I had enough time and I devoted my whole time to know these things. Don't say that I am perfect, I don't say that. I may goof, make mistakes too. There is no perfect human being. To be perfect, is to be perfectly boring. There is only one who is perfect, the Divine One. Perfect is a word that we do not find in reality. But when you devote time to learn something, you will discover many skills which nobody taught you. When you are doing something with concentration and persistence, that skill of yours will lead you to greater skills; you will attain greater heights.

ॐ

Chapter 6

Contemplation, Prayer and Repentance

Mantra 6

एष सर्वेश्वर एष सर्वज्ञ एषोऽन्तर्याम्येष
योनिः सर्वस्य प्रभवाप्ययौ हि भूतानाम् ॥ ६ ॥

*Esha sarveshvara esha sarva-jna esho'ntaryamy
-esha yonih sarvasya prabhavapyayau hi bhutanam.*

Esha sarveshvara
(The experiencer of these states is) the Lord of all.

esha sarva-jna esho'ntaryamy-esha yonih
This one is all-knowing, directs everything from within and is the womb of all.

sarvasya prabhavapyayau hi bhutanam
All things originate from and dissolve into this.

There are two philosophical approaches: one, that leads you from gross to grosser and then to the grossest and the other which leads you from gross to subtle, to subtler, and then to the subtlest aspect.

Mandukya Upanishad is of the second type. It does not talk much about God. It's a very practical Upanishad. It directly leads you to the innermost center of consciousness, from where consciousness flows eternally, and bestows freedom.

This Upanishad will lead you from the external world to the internal world. You are not satisfied with the idea that God is everywhere, that you know. Is there any Bible which does not say so? Then why are you running around the world, going to this temple, going to that synagogue, to that church, why? It is because you have not been trained to understand that the Lord is within you. You think you are very small, so you think that God is also small. How can such a big God, great God, live in such a small body? The day that you come to know that you are a living temple, a living shrine, you will know the wonder of life. There are not just seven or eight wonders in the world. The greatest of all wonders, wonder of wonders, is that this finite human being, this small vessel, has infinity within it. Wherever this vessel moves, infinity moves with it. What a wonderful thing! That's why a human being is considered to be great. According to the Koran, he is called *Ashraful Makhlukhat,* highest of all creatures. For him there is joy in abundance. In the Bible, it is said that man has been created in the image of God. The day we come to know that we are a shrine, there will be great joy. God is in me!

We can understand life practically according to the theme of this Upanishad, first by understanding vishwa, the gross world. But who is trying to analyze, understand and experience? Who experiences that this is the waking state, not a dream? There is only one experiencer called Atman. That Atman is within you and you are that Atman. First a sadhaka, an aspirant, will have to understand that, that which you call God, or Absolute Truth or Reality, is not far away from you, but is within you. Thou art That. The experiencer of this external universe, Vaishvanara, according to this Upanishad, is the same as the one who experiences Taijasa, the dreaming state, the one who experiences Prajna the sleeping state, and the one whose permanent abode is in Turiya. It is the same One who is experiencing all these states. There are not two gods, there cannot be. If God dwells everywhere, if he is omnipresent, omnipotent, and omniscient, then that power, that great Truth, that Absolute Reality who is considered to be God, can only be one, not two. There cannot be, there is no space, for two. There is no space for God to move; because he's everywhere, where can he move? Then the question comes, where are you? Where do you exist? You apparently exist in one of these experiences, waking, dreaming or sleeping, but your true existence is the Absolute Reality. Your abode is actually Turiya, the fourth. You are a citizen of many countries, many worlds, waking, dreaming and sleeping, but actually you are the dweller of the fourth state.

I do not understand how you can feel that you and God are two different entities. The moment you do that, you have insulted the Lord, who is the inner dweller, who is everywhere. You are separating yourself from That; it's a great insult to such a great majesty. You constantly insult such a great majesty, that's why you suffer. May you learn not to insult that great majesty! So what is your duty? Your duty is to establish that supreme I, which is indicated as Turiya, in place of that little I, mere I, which is called ego, because ego has separated you from the whole. Meditation will help you, but in the method of meditation you will also have to include vichara, or contemplation. You will have to learn to have an inner dialogue, a pleasant dialogue, with yourself.

Contemplation is entering into a dialogue with yourself. You can lie to others but you can never lie to yourself, never. So when you enter into a dialogue with yourself, you will know many things, but don't get discouraged and defeated. Deep down within you, there are two diverse things. One enters into a dialogue with the mind. Tukaram, one of the sages, prays to his mind first. Have you ever heard of praying to your own mind? Tulsidasa, another sage, prayed to the devil first. *"Durjanam prathamam vande."* He said, "I bow to that which is creating this obstacle, please, don't create obstacles for me; I bow to you." It means you are being humble; you can reach there with humility, not with arrogance, not with intellect. "I know nothing; I might know something as far as the world is concerned, but I know nothing, as far as God is concerned. I am a fool. What to do? Ninety-nine point nine percent of people in the world are fools, and there is no Bible for fools. Therefore, Lord protect me, help me." So Tukaram says, *"Manah sarvada bhakta panthe vijayate."* He enters into a dialogue with his mind, "O mind, why are you roaming around, why are you torturing me? Be on the path of righteousness. O mind, allow my tongue to speak only what is right." Sometimes you speak something, but you think something different; this creates a split personality. Don't do that. When you enter into a dialogue with your mind, that type of contemplation helps you a lot.

Then there is something else, very striking, very important: Prayer and repentance. These should be understood very properly. Before going to bed, you should pray to the Lord who is within you, who is the experiencer of all these states. "O inner dweller,

Lord of my life, and the Lord of this universe, help me." What help? Don't ask for some worldly thing, ask for strength. Always ask for strength, because He alone has strength, no one else has strength. Any strength that you have is nothing compared to His strength. "Give me strength, O Lord, so that I may go through this disorganized, huge, unmanageable procession of life." This way you will come in touch with the finer part of yourself. It means that if you have determination, you'll find the way. If you are selfless and strong, and if you are trying to do something, it will be done. If I do something, nobody is going to help me. Nature helps. Help comes from an unknown quarter. Unknown means, the Lord; Truth always helps ultimately.

Christ never said I beg your pardon, please don't crucify me. Did he say that? No, he was crucified, but look at his strength. He was so one with his conviction, that there was no pain. When conviction has gone beyond pain and pleasure, there can be no pain. For you and me, if we are crucified, in five minutes time, we'll say "Ok, Ok, we are very sorry, please set us free." He never said that. He didn't care. Death of the body was nothing for him with the conviction that he had. Prayer can lead to that conviction.

What is repentance? Prayer and repentance are two wings of the same bird that is trying to fly from here to Brahman. When you are doing something wrong, you know it. But when others say you are doing wrong, you feel bad. Why do you feel bad? Why do you do it when you know that it is bad? That which is accepted as bad by you, and by others, is bad. What do you do in such a case? Repent. Repent means not to repeat. Decide that you are not going to repeat it. Many times you slip, but then again, be strong. Learn to fight; life is a battle, a Kurukshetra. *Vira bhogya vasundhara*, only the courageous can enjoy this world, not the weak. Prayer and repentance, every day. "Lord, give me strength, so that nothing deviates me from my path, help me O Lord." Don't condemn yourself; otherwise it's a total disaster. So prayer gives you strength, while repentance purifies you. When you determine, "I will not do it again," you are free.

Do you know what is worse than killing the innocent? I can prove that you all are murderers and murderesses. You are killing your conscience all the time; you are not listening to it. The greatest of all sins, actually there is only one sin, and that is to kill your conscience. Keep your conscience alive. If you commit a mistake, don't be flattened like a ball of clay; try to be that ball which bounces back, ball of rubber. Prayer and repentance are both essential.

A human being is bound by a law, and that law is that he cannot live without doing action. So, when he does actions, he continues doing them, he cannot come out; he is caught in a whirlpool. So there is only one way of being free from the bondage of karma, which is the first freedom you need.

Let us count freedoms one by one. First freedom is freedom from the bondage of karma, by doing selfless action. What is this unit, of family, meant for? Wife should do karma for husband, husband should do karma for wife; they are doing karma themselves, but fruits should be given to each other, and they both should give the fruits to their children. Do this experiment, and you'll find, expansion, freedom in the world. Without giving the fruits of your actions, you can never be free. So learn to give the fruits of your actions to the people with whom you live. That's one freedom.

There is another bondage, and that is created by the mind. May you engage your mind with japa, repeating the name of God, with prayer. May you meditate, make your mind one-pointed and inward; and thus attain Turiya, be happy and free.

Tell me, you go to a temple and pray according to your religion; why do you pray again and again? Because you think that your prayer was not valid, it was not heard, thus you are doing it again and again. Learning to give is the right kind of prayer. May you understand that giving is a great prayer. It gives you freedom immediately, it gives you delight, it makes others happy. You are not giving to another human being; you are giving to the Lord, who is in every human being. That's called prayer through action, prayer through karma. So your karma will never create bondage if it becomes a prayer. That's my point, prayer will never create bondage. May you learn to give, starting with your own family, at home. The home is a great temple, where live all the gods, learning to help each other, learning to love each other, learning to be free. That family is admirable, whose head becomes an example, faced with all the diversities, yet maintaining that unity underneath.

Now let me tell you something; if you are not on talking terms with your neighbors, how can you love your neighbors? If you do not love your neighbors, do not have cordial relationships with your neighbors, you will never understand them, they will never understand you. So is the case with yourself. If you do not learn to love yourself, appreciate and admire yourself, if you go on condemning yourself, how will you know yourself? If you go on condemning your neighbors, how will you know your neighbors? How can you say that you love your neighbors, and if you do not love your neighbors why should they love you?

From where have you learned to condemn yourself? You learn because you commit mistakes. That which you think is good today, you may consider to be a mistake tomorrow. And that goes on piling up. It becomes a catalogue of mistakes and then it creates a complex. No, learn to forgive yourself too. If you don't do that, you'll go on condemning yourself and you'll create a living hell for yourself. Don't do that. A human being is the highest of all known species, one considered to be very close to the Ultimate Reality, once he or she learns to realize.

First of all from the very beginning you will have to learn a word called love. I told you just now, if you do not love yourself, if you go on condemning yourself, if you go on hating yourself, no God on earth, no angel in the heavens can help you. You will have to have one thing, and that is called grace of the Self, remember this. If you offer all your human responsibilities to God, a human being is crippled. That is not called self surrender, that is called being lazy and irresponsible. Work with the determination that you can do it, you will do it, you have to do it; then you are bound to do it.

So may you learn to understand one thing: You should make every human effort that's possible. When human efforts are exhausted, then dawns the divine aspect, that's called grace or descending force. On whom does He choose to shower His grace? He chooses one who has made his efforts, all human efforts with firm faith, with complete dedication, with all his mind, action and speech; such a one is graced. To such a one, dawns the descending force. There is a meeting point here, the Lord meets the human being. The Lord of life, Truth, Absolute Truth meets the human being. You are still a human being and yet you meet God. Christ met Absolute Reality, he did not become a Buddhist. Buddha became enlightened, he did not become a Christian. So don't be afraid that you will be changed. Don't be afraid of change; you'll be transformed and that's what you need.

ॐ

Chapter 7

The Fourth State, Turiya

Mantra 7

नान्तःप्रज्ञं न बहिष्प्रज्ञं नोभयतः
प्रज्ञं न प्रज्ञानघनं न प्रज्ञं नाप्रज्ञम् ।
अदृष्टमव्यवहार्यमग्राह्यमलक्षणम्
अचिन्त्यमव्यपदेश्यमेकात्मप्रत्ययसारं
प्रपञ्चोपशमं शान्तं शिवमद्वैतं
चतुर्थं मन्यन्ते स आत्मा स विज्ञेयः ॥ ७ ॥

Nantah-prajnam na bahih-prajnam nobhayatah-prajnam na prajnana-ghanam na prajnam na aprajnam. Adrishtam-avyavaharyam-agrahyam-alakshanam-achintyam-avyapadeshyam-ekatama-pratyaya-saram prapanchopa shamam shantam shivam advaitam chaturtam manyate sa atma sa vijneyah.

Nantah-prajnam na bahih-prajnam nobhayatah-prajnam
Consciousness is neither inward turned nor outward turned nor both.

na prajnana-ghanam na prajnam na aprajnam.
It is not undifferentiated, it is beyond cognition and non-cognition.

Adrishtam-avyavaharyam-agrahyam-alakshanam-achintyam-avyapadeshyam
Not experienced by the senses, nor known by comparison or inference, incomprehensible, unthinkable and indescribable,

ekatama-pratyaya-saram prapanchopa shamam
pure consciousness, the real Self, the cessation of all phenomena,

shantam shivam advaitam
tranquil, all-blissful, one without a second,

chaturtam manyate sa atma sa vijneyah.
this fourth state (Turiya), the Atma (Real Self) is to be realized.

I pray to the divinity in you. Do you understand why we bring our hands together in the gesture called praying hands? What do you mean by praying hands? Two hands meet, jiva meets Brahman. Your prayer should be so intense that you become One, you are lost in Brahman consciousness. So greeting others thus, means that I pray to the Brahman in you. It's not a gesture meant for any human being. It's a gesture for the Brahman that you see, you recognize, realize in others. When you start doing this, then you cannot fight with anyone, you cannot hate anyone, you cannot despise anyone, you cannot injure, hurt or kill anyone. That's what it means.

Even after having rest in the blissful state of deep sleep, a human being wakes up, comes out. Why does he come out? He wants to experience the joy that he had in deep sleep. It means that the joy experienced through our senses is better than that experienced in any other way in the external world. So this external world experience is not invalid. We want to have all our experiences here. I want to see God with my own two eyes. If God exists somewhere, I want to see him. If God exists somewhere, I want to smell him. If God exists somewhere, I want to touch him. This is the human tendency. So the Upanishads say, experiencing is not limited to the waking, dream and deep sleep states; there is a state beyond the three states which is called Turiya, the highest, where there is no sadness, where there is no pain. Of course sadness and pain disappear when you are in deep sleep. Who is your son, who is your father, who is your beloved, who is your lover? In deep sleep, you forget all that. It means that in this state you have to experience aloneness. You are all alone there. You cannot say to your wife, "Let's both go consciously into deep sleep and be aware when we are sleeping." No, you become aware only when you are awake. That sleep experience is your personal experience. Your dream is your personal dream; it is not your wife's dream or your child's dream. Your sleep is your personal sleep. You go to a personal chamber, but it is not a universal experience. It lacks universality, because we are all not there.

Now we want a joy which is experienced by the whole universe. Truth is that truth which encompasses the whole universe, which is beneficial universally, which is a universal truth. A personal truth, an individual truth is not considered to be totally valid. The joy which you experience in deep sleep is higher than the joy of the waking and dream states. But the yogis say that there is a state beyond, in which the joy we experience is higher than that of the three other states. It is a permanent joy unlike the fleeting, temporary joy of the other states. The yogis say that when you go to the highest state you will experience the whole universe; when you attain that summit, that peak, you will see everything from there, all around, above and below. Turiya is that final state the yogis strive to attain in order to achieve complete bliss, in order to fulfill their one single ambition, that of attaining Absolute Truth.

At present, your now is not now, it's your past or your future. Your mind always goes to the grooves of the past, or sometimes tries to fathom the future through your imagination. If you learn how to keep your mind here and now, the future can be called into the now, because during that time, your mental capacity, your mental horizon expands. That is possible.

Meditation should not be colored with cultural or religious values. There is nothing like Hindu meditation, Christian meditation or Buddhist meditation. Meditation is meditation. It's a method of going to the center of consciousness from where consciousness flows on various degrees and grades. How to make the body still, so that during that time your muscles take complete rest? How to breathe properly, in a harmonious way so that body and breath coordinate perfectly and your nervous system gets perfect rest? How to lead your mind to a state of equilibrium even for a few minutes, so that your brain and thinking process remain at rest? This way you can lead a healthy life in a comprehensive way, holistically, this is my point. We will consider this systematic approach. When you sit for meditation, suppose you receive a hunch. And then you expect to receive it again the next day, but you don't, and you wonder, "Yesterday I received a hunch that came true, but today I am not receiving such hunches. What's the matter?" Perhaps when you received that hunch, your mind was calm; perhaps you were in a state of tranquility, prepared to receive that knowledge which is already in the infinite library within you. Today you are not in that situation. But if you systematically practice, you can receive every day that knowledge which does not flow through the mind but flows through inner vision. There is a method of meditation for that. Well, there is only one thing that I cannot do for you, and that's called meditation. You will have to do meditation for yourself. I can cook for you, I can wash your bottom, I can change your diapers, I can clean your room, I can do your laundry, but I cannot meditate for you. You will have to meditate for yourself. As the Buddha said, "Ye, light thy own lamp. Nobody will give you salvation." You are an individual, you do your individual karmas, you have your individual mind, you have individual thinking, you have individual emotions, you know yourself best and only you can know yourself. You have to establish a state of equilibrium and tranquility which gives you peace.

As I told you, three aspects of Om are considered to be waking, dream, and deep sleep. But the Vedas explain the four padas, four feet of the eternal, in a different way also. The Veda says, *Pado asya vishwani bhutani tripadsya amritandhuve.* The entire universe comes with one pada, one aspect. It is the only aspect of Brahman, of the Absolute Truth. What happened to tripada, to the other three aspects? So there was a conference of sages and wise men, and nobody could explain that. Because it is written, *tripadsya amrit-*

andhuve. Three padas, three aspects are eternal. So one of the old sages got up and said it's really very simple. Sat, chit, and ananda, that is existence, consciousness and bliss, are the three padas. These are three aspects of the Absolute and one aspect is called Maya's aspect, namely this whole universe.

One of the Upanishads says that Pranava (another name for Om), is setu or bridge. According to Patanjali, the codifier of yoga science, if you have learnt to establish a bridge from this shore to the other shore with the help of Pranava, you have accomplished your task. It teaches you meditation without an object. Why are you not improving, why are you not deepening your meditation? Why does your mind not get concentrated and attain the next step, meditative step? Because your method is poor, it's shallow. Why do you experience frustration when you love someone? Because of your incorrect method of loving, because your love is poor. So the scriptures say that when you learn to love and learn to tread the path of light and love without objects, then you learn to attain that final goal which is called Turiya and finally you attain it. In this method you don't use any object, no picture of a guru or deity, or messenger, no objects.

Now, you will find that it is very difficult for you to concentrate your mind without an object. Mind always wants to lean on something. Who taught you to lean on something all the time, to depend on something all the time? You talk of drug dependency or alcohol dependency or some other dependency. No, no, these dependencies are nothing. You are suffering on account of a serious crisis. That crisis is a spiritual crisis caused by that dependency created in you by your mind. You will never find mind being independent. Never, not for a second! It is always dependent on something. Watch your mind and see.

Is there any moment when your mind is free from an object or from an image? No. We have to learn to make our mind independent first; free from imagery, free from objects, free from imaginations; only then will the mind be capable of fathoming the deeper levels of our being, the subtle levels of our being.

Why are you not successful in meditation? You do the technical things correctly. You sit down, you have learnt to keep your head, neck and trunk in a straight line, you have attained stillness of body. Then you attend to breath. After that, you do not know what to do, because something more subtle comes up. You do not know how to withdraw your mind because you are in the habit of employing the senses. How can the senses be withdrawn during that time, so that your mind instead of flowing to the external world starts turning within? So what you actually need to do is to make your mind inward, to make your mind one-pointed. The mind should be both inward directed and one-pointed. You can make the mind one-pointed, using one of the senses, but through that sense, we are making the mind externally directed, though one-pointed. For meditation, you need to make the mind one-pointed, of course, but at the same time, directed inward. That's what this mantra says.

As long as there is attachment, no practice is possible, no sadhana is accomplished, no meditation is fruitful. You are doing incomplete meditation, meditation which is not supported by the right philosophy. That is why that meditation technique does not lead you anywhere. It gives you a small glimpse. It can create an escape for you, it can give you some calmness, some healing balm, but it will not lead you in the right direction.

I want you to understand meditation properly. It's a very interesting, healthy, and helpful subject. The word meditation comes from the same root as the word 'medical' and means 'to attend to.' As a good doctor attends to his patient seriously and lovingly, so in meditation, the meditator should attend to the object of his meditation regularly and effectively, so that he removes all barriers and goes ahead and attains the final liberation.

Meditating for five or ten minutes in a quiet corner of your house is very good. But that meditation should be brought into action. Meditation in action means you should learn to do your actions with full attention. For lack of attention, you stumble in your house where you have lived for 50 years. Why is attention a very important part of meditation? If you want to attain success in meditation, you have to pay attention to your actions. Why are you doing this particular work? Why are you doing this action? Do it attentively and you will reap the fruits of your actions the way you want. You are discontented, because you expect too much and you do too little. You did not get what you should, by your estimation. Either you have learned to imagine baselessly, or you have not performed your actions accurately. When you attend to the entire process of action, then you will not be disappointed or frustrated. I always say, do not be satisfied but remain contented. If you are satisfied, there is no motivation. You will not be motivated to do something. But, dissatisfaction comes when you start doing something. Contentment comes when you have already done something. Most of us aspire to do something, expect to do something and do not do it with our full attention, and hence do not get the fruits according to our desires. What do we get? We get frustrated, discontented. Well, the action has been performed; now you cannot do anything about it. Why are you discontented? "It's my habit," people say. To remain discontented and frustrated will create many, many diseases; will make you sick, will rob you of cheerfulness, will rob your peace; therefore, learn to be contented. And pay attention when you perform your actions, do it with full attention. You will find that you have improved in all fields. You may be a doctor, a scientist, an accountant, or a yogi; but whatever you do, do it with full attention and this is the first step on the path of meditation in action.

First of all, you should decide why you want to sit like this and breathe like this; why do you want to do all this? If you do not know, then your mind will ask you why are you doing all this. What to do next? Before going to bed, sit down, and watch your mind, by focusing your mind on the space between the two eyebrows. This is called ajna chakra. This word, ajna, means a little knowledge. That which is considered knowledge, though it is little, is received by focusing your mind on the space between the two eyebrows. Many of you strain your eyes and eyebrows, because you have read it somewhere. This is injurious. Fix your mind between the two eyebrows. Close your eyes, ask your mind to focus at the point between your eyebrows. What will happen? As soon as you do it, with your eyes closed and your senses not in touch with the external world, those impressions which you have stored within, will start coming before you, one by one.

I want to lead you towards subtler realms of your unconscious mind. So first you should learn to observe your thinking process. If I observe something with attachment, that is not called observation, no. You have to observe as a judge, you should not observe something as a culprit, that's the point. What should your attitude be when you observe your thinking process? You should decide before you observe, that no matter what thought comes up, you will not get involved with it. If it is a bad thought that hurts me, let it come, it should not hurt me. If it is a good thought, it should not please me, it's a thought. You should keep your mind very clear no matter which thought comes.

Most religious books of the world promise to introduce you to God, but not the Bhagavad Gita. The theme of the Gita is to make you a super human, stithadhihi. So Gita has given birth to behavioral science. *Stithadhihi kim prabhahshet kima seet vrajate kim.* The student is asking his teacher, "What are you going to make out of me?" The teacher replies, "I want to make you stithadhihi, I want to make you a super human, a perfect human." Not perfectly boring, but perfect human. Sometimes this perfection business can be perfectly boring!

I tell you something. It's a curse to become a swami because I have to live according to your expectations and I cannot live according to my own nature. Swamiji should not move, Swamiji should sit like this. So before you come to see a swami, you have a notion in your mind about a swami. You fix that notion in your mind when you come to see a swami. And if, in real life, that swami does not come up to your expectations, he's not a swami. So the poor gurus also face serious problems. Our relationship should be based on truth, on selflessness, on pure love. You can straight away tell your teacher, you are being selfish. Perhaps he will learn something from you. You know, a teacher learns more from his students than from his teacher.

Initially the tradition was a father-son lineage. The best you have, you hand over to your children. There was a spiritual succession and that spiritual succession traveled from father to son. After Shuka, in our tradition, the succession changed from father-son, to guru-disciple, and that continues even today. Your disciple is more than your son. Sometimes a son is not capable of receiving what you have, but a disciple is, according to the tradition, dearer to his teacher. If you go to someone's house, which door do you go through first? Do you go in through the bathroom to get in? No. You straight away go through the front door. Always be straightforward, ask questions, useful questions, that's all. Those who live near a temple are more sinful than others, because they lose the value of the deva, the deity, who dwells in the temple.

So is the case with students. Students constantly want to receive all the experiences that the teacher has received from his teacher. I have nothing of my own to give you; I am offering you that which I was given by those whom I regard with great reverence, because of the blessings and happiness they bestowed on me. When you listen to somebody's lectures, he's only a lecturer. When you learn to listen to him repeatedly, you want to learn more from him, he becomes your teacher. When you want him to impart more subtle things, subtleties of spirituality, you become a disciple. There are steps for that.

So the Bhagavad Gita explains three or four things you should observe before you accept some-body as your guru. How does he speak? Does he speak in a selfless manner all the time or is he selfish and wants this and that? How does he sit? If he has not learned to sit, he has not meditated, simple. When I was asked to go see other teachers, my master said,

"First, see the posture of your teacher. Can he sit for a long time in one posture without any problem? It means he has done meditation." Kabira, a poet and sage, always talked about asana, posture. Here posture does not mean headstand or shoulderstand. Posture means the way you have learned to sit. If your posture is sthira and sukha, steady and comfortable, it means you have practiced. Then you learn to listen to such a teacher. My Master never told me to go to universities, to go and listen to people who have doctorates and D.Litt.s. No, discard that. Dark words will not impart knowledge, for they are dark themselves. From where will they shed light? How does he sit, how does he talk? How does he walk? Suppose you want to buy a diamond. You have to see all the qualities of the diamond before you buy it. So also, with selecting a teacher.

Now, there are two views on this. In Islamic literature it is said, if your teacher asks you to dip your jainawaz in liquor, do it. Jainawaz means meditation carpet, carpet used for Nawaz, prayer. But in yoga science, in our ancient tradition it is not said like that. Prepare yourself, so that you know what are the qualities, subtle qualities, of the teacher. As the Gita says, "How does he sit, how does he talk, how does he walk?" This reflects a particular discipline that he has gone through. If he has not gone through that discipline, don't waste your time. It is easier to meet an alchemist who can turn copper into gold than to meet a spiritual teacher who can transform your life.

So when you first learn to use your conscious mind, a small part of the totality of mind used in the waking state, you make use of the resources you have. Mind is an instrument; consciousness is flow of chetana, which is energy along with knowledge.

Remember the energy of the mind does not belong to the mind; mind is only an instrument. What is the brain then? This simile will teach you the difference between brain, mind and nervous system. The network of wires is the nervous system, the bulb is the brain, and the electricity that is flowing through it is called the mind. Now I may have a good nervous system and a good brain. But if my mind is somewhere else, what good is that? For mind is expressed through the brain. But what does it express? It projects the power of consciousness that is there. Mind is like a projector, projects the external world. From where has this external world, Vaishvanara, come? What happens to it? Does it last forever? When we see that everything is changing, we know that a time will come when they will no longer exist. All namas and rupas, names and forms, will dissolve sooner or later.

Some forms last for a few years, other forms may last for more years. Once they are dissolved, what happens to them? Even this form that is called the universe is going to change one day. What will happen? It will go to annihilation. But even in annihilation, the ancient Vedic scriptures, shrutis say, *Surya chandramasodata yata purvam akalpayet.* The sun, moon, stars, this whole universe will at some point go to its resting place, Brahman, the summum bonum of life; then ages later, the universe will again re-manifest exactly the way it used to be. It's a scientific law. If you have a mango seed, no matter how it is stored, when it germinates, it will bring forth only mango. In reality, nothing happens. This is all Brahman, a gross aspect of Brahman.

The impressions that you carry in your heart and mind can distort your actions, beliefs, faith, and create a new faith for you, thus changing your philosophy, your living, everything. These impressions need to be examined. Remember that fears need to be examined, for fears are responsible for accidents, all accidents. Accidents are self-invited; let me assure you of this. There is nothing like an accident, this is all determined by you. You are not aware. This happens in your unconscious mind, and your unconscious mind creates the circumstances for the accident to take place. You have control, a little control, only on your conscious mind during the waking state, but you have no control over your unconscious mind. To bring the unconscious mind under conscious control is a great achievement of yogic science.

I took a physicist under a banyan tree. The banyan tree is a very big tree that spreads its roots over a large area, even bigger than a large building. I wanted to examine the impact of physics on his mind. He was a doctorate in physics. I said to him, "This is a very old tree. There lives a ghost under this tree. I have seen it. Do you believe in ghosts?" He replied, "I don't believe in ghosts. Though you are a friend of mine, I have to tell you that while you have your own field of specialization, my field is different and I don't believe in things like ghosts." I tried to convince him, but he rejected my beliefs. Next day, I created circumstances that forced him to pass by that tree at night, when he was all alone. I was sitting nearby to observe what happens to him. He never used to say Ram, Ram, Lord, Lord, but suddenly from his mouth came, "Om, Ram, Ram, Ram, Ram, Om, Ram, Ram." He was afraid. He said he did not believe in ghosts but he remembered my words. These words left some impression in his unconscious mind, and when his conscious mind could not deal with the situation, the unconscious mind came forward because of my suggestion that there was a ghost. Physics says that there is nothing like a ghost, but the swami says that there is a ghost and he has seen it. With great fear and difficulty he passed by the tree. Then I suddenly stood up. He wasn't expecting me there and he mistook me for a ghost and fainted. I consoled him saying, "Come on, I am your friend. There is no ghost." It took him some time to compose himself.

Meditation is that conscious method of turning the mind inward. Between two thoughts, there will be space, so there will be time, and there will be causation. If there is only one thought, then there is no space, there is no time, there is no causation. So, in meditation, you do not want three or four or ten or twenty thoughts; you want only one thought for a long time; that is called meditation. When concentration is strengthened so that only one thought persists for a long time, that is called meditation. So in meditation, mind is not conditioned by time, space or causation. As long as the mind is conditioned by time, it is not meditation, it is something else. You are making efforts to meditate, but you have not attained it if there are many thoughts. Suppose you are doing japa. If you constantly do japa and nothing intervenes, then it is meditation. If thoughts intervene, then it is not meditation. The intervening thoughts have a space, and then the mind is affected by time, space and causation. So what you do in meditation is to prolong a single thought.

Is meditation a mere escape? Is meditation therapeutic for you? Is meditation a form of experimentation for you? Are you trying to explore something, or are you doing meditation because Swami Rama told you to do? That's a very dangerous situation if you are meditating because I am telling you to do meditation. Then that is not instruction in meditation, it is called instruction in hypnosis. I am explaining to you the benefits of meditation. If you understand the benefits you should learn to experiment. In the beginning, take meditation as an experiment and later, truthfully ask yourself if the method was helpful for you or not? We have all done experiments. Only if we walk up to that gate, will we see that gate. As an experiment, find out if remaining very still, making breath serene and calming the mind, brings you peace. Can that peace be obtained in any other way? When you start doing this sort of experiment, then you do not need any outer agency to support or validate your experience. Learn to do meditation, independently. Whether you are a good or bad person, happy or sad person, you should do meditation. No need of becoming miserable. If others make you miserable then you are weak. It means weakness creates misery. Learn to have inner strength; external strength is a good support for external life but internal strength will help you when you need it.

There is one simple sentence in Ramayana that says, *Dhiraj, dharma, mitra aur nari, apta kala par kyo jari.* It is a general indication that when in need, a man should test dhiraj, his courage, his dharma or conviction, his mitra or trusted friend and nari, his wife whom he loves. Why do you test them? Suppose you are drowning and you are depending on someone to save you and that person doesn't save you, then what is your fate? You should learn to test them, at least once or twice. First to be tested is not the woman you love, but dhiraj, your courage. Do you have inner courage? What have you done to create inner courage? If you go on condemning yourself, you will never have inner courage, no matter how many supports you have in the external world. Inner courage will come when you learn to be happy in solitude. A mother sometimes says, "Children now you go to sleep, let me be alone for a moment." She loves her children, she cannot live without husband, children, home and everything, but still she says, "Let me be away from everybody for sometime." There is a desire to be all alone to enjoy that bliss which you find only when you are all alone and not with others. You do not need a group to make you happy. Every individual has that desire to be alone for sometime, that's why you meditate. You want to reach that point.

So I told you that only a small portion of the mind functions during the waking state and we spend all our time and energy in cultivating that portion of mind which remains awake. So we understand how to utilize that conscious part of mind for our external needs. We do not know how to use that conscious part of mind to turn within. When we start doing this consciously, it is called the first step in meditation. We do not want the mind to dissipate our energy, which of course comes from the center of consciousness, through the senses. As soon as you wake up, you'll find that your senses gradually become active and then you become active. All the activities in your body are because of your mind and senses; but all the knowledge in your body is because of the center of consciousness within. A human being is not perfect. He remains dissatisfied, and remains unfulfilled, because he is utilizing only a small part of the inner resources given to him by Providence, by Nature.

Now let us go a little deeper. I told you there is a transitional state, called unmani awastha, between waking and dreaming which is realized and experienced by meditators. Sometimes while meditating, suddenly, something happens to you, and you touch that dimension. After a few minutes, you realize you did not know where you were. You were neither dreaming nor were you brooding on the objects of the world. You had an experience of nothingness. Most gurus, teachers and preceptors tell you not to allow your mind to slip into that state of nothingness. Your mind should be under your control all the time. If you allow your mind to slip like that, then you will form a habit and the mind will no longer be under your control. It's just like flying a kite where you are just holding the string but you do not know what has happened to the kite. That unmani state of mind is a sort of discovery of the unknown; it's just like going through a black hole. No one knows what it is. When the yogis discovered it, they called it absent mind-edness, it's not at all productive. They tried to understand unmani awastha, that state of mind which leads you to unproductivity, where you cannot become creative, but you just waste your time and energy. So, that unmani awastha should not be cultivated. It can lead your mind to hallucination. All hallucinations that come into your mind are because of that unmani awastha, where you are not attending to your object of meditation, the focal point. Many people, for lack of control and awareness, for lack of understanding, form the habit of hallucinating. And when hallucination reaches a further stage, then what does it become? It becomes a sickness and then you say, he or she has the habit of hallucinating, hallucinates all the time. Therefore, unmani awastha is not considered to be helpful to the student. Teachers warn you not to waste your time, not to allow the mind to slip into that unhealthy state.

When your mind is one-pointed, you cannot imagine how much power you have. What is it? It is called sankalpa shakti, power of determination. If your determination leads your mind one-pointedly, you can do anything. You have so much power, the power of determination. You should learn to utilize that power of determination which is called sankalpa shakti, which is the first thing that is taught.

You have all heard of a method called mesmerism. Actually the method was not discovered by psychologists, but by a Mr. Mesmer who was lost in the jungles of Africa. He did not know what to do at night, lost in a dense forest. So he took shelter under a tree on which he found a huge snake looking upwards. The moment the snake looked upwards, the birds fell down, even monkeys fell down. He said, "There is something in those eyes. This snake has powerful eyes." Then he said, "Why only the snake, why can't I have such eyes?" He started training his eyes. He did not know anything about the yogic practice called trataka. In yoga, this is an ancient practice. There are some rules. Don't practice it unless you are told to do so. The yogis gaze at a light, a candle whose flame does not flicker. Slowly the time is increased. The day you can do it for half an hour, you'll find that if you look towards somebody, electricity will pass into his body. If you look towards a cat or dog, they will become motionless because of the power in your eyes. No, this is not the power of the eyes alone. Your mind becomes concentrated and that mind is focused through one avenue called the eyes. It's not only mind's power, it is the power of your individual soul. You do not know how powerful you are from within. Love is considered to be a great power, the power of powers, provided you are not selfish. You just learn to give selflessly, that's a great power. It depends on which way you use your powers.

Before you do any ritual, any spiritual practice or any religious ritual, you first have to build your sankalpa shakti, willpower. It reminds one to compose oneself before doing any rituals, any puja, any prayer, any meditation, any contemplation. In rituals, the first thing the priest will tell you, is to make a sankalpa, a determination. In this sankalpa ritual, the priest will lead you to remember your ancestors, "Come great sages, great seers." Why? It is to stimulate the question, "When I come from a great tradition, why can't I achieve that greatness?" So then, you are inspired to remember all the good you have done in your past. Those who have studied the Ishopanishad know that its mantras say that while departing, a soul, an individual soul, should learn to remember all that it has done, all the good things it has done, because those good deeds will not create sadness, depression, fear in the mind when going through the transition. So far you have been preparing yourself to be comfortable in the external world, to be in a world full of means, which is essential, but now, you are preparing yourself to go through the period of transition. Sooner or later we all have to go through that transition. Look at this strange thing, we all have to depart one day, yet we never believe that we will die. Do you know why? Why do you believe that you will not die? Because there is no death for eternity and you are a child of eternity. The soul never dies, which you know unconsciously. The best part of you never dies. That which changes, goes to death and decay, that alone dies. So why are you afraid of dying? From where does this fear come? This fear comes from ignorance. Scientifically, nothing dies. Death only means change. Death does not mean complete annihilation.

Before you do meditation, build your sankalpa shakti; I will do it, I can do it, I have to do it, I am fully equipped to do it, it's my birthright; this is called willpower. But if you are not very sure, you will be wasting your time and energy, don't do anything.

First know the technique fully, and then practice it. In meditation, no emergency will arise forcing you to come out of meditation.

Let me tell you something. This I witnessed personally. There was an old couple who decided to stay in the city of Brindavan upon retirement. And I was there, in the same city, the same lane, staying next to their house. Their grandson came to visit them. A woman naturally gets attached to things, because she is more responsible, as far as worldly affairs are concerned. Men are not responsible by nature. The husband had long before resigned his job and all his concerns, and dedicated himself totally to the Lord. When he was sitting in puja or meditation, he had given strict instructions that he should not be disturbed, no matter what happened in the world. Somebody dies, somebody is born, but nobody should disturb him. One day, that child, the grandson, fell down from the fourth floor onto the lane which was full of rocks. There is no chance of survival if somebody falls down from the fourth floor, especially a child. When the child fell down from the fourth floor, the grandmother got up and under the great agony, anxiety and pain that she felt, she called out to her husband, "Old man, get up, what is this puja! Take him to the doctor." He smiled and continued his worship. Again she said, "You stupid fellow, our grandson has fallen down from the fourth floor; you hypocrite, you heard me tell you this and yet you are sitting in meditation." He said, "As long as I am in meditation, nothing bad can happen. But something might happen if I come out; he might die. I had better remain in meditation." But the woman wouldn't listen. In India we have a type of broom, called jharu, to sweep the floor. She brought the jharu and started beating her husband with it. Sometimes, husband-wife relationship can lead to such fights too, even fist fights! She started beating him, but he did not react. Finally, she kicked him, but even then he did nothing. When he wouldn't get up, she went to the kitchen, where the fire was burning, and picked up one of the burning sticks of firewood and started hitting him with it. The poor fellow suffered many burns on his body, I saw the burns, but he wouldn't get up. Finally, in her anger, she started weeping and shouting. After half an hour he came out of his meditation and said, "Nothing has happened to our grandson, but you wanted to kill him. You also injured me and almost killed me." He was so firm in his faith that when one is in meditation nothing bad will ever happen. What emergency can you have? Do you want to protect yourself from God? Do you want to protect yourself from the blissful state? Do you want to protect yourself from Turiya? Do you think that by coming out of meditation, the world will protect you? The world outside is a most unsafe place. The greatest enemies that you have are in your home, are those who claim to love you; strangers are not your enemies. Who makes you unhappy? Those who love you, those who claim to love you. Once you understand this, then you go and find a refuge, a shelter, in your inner world, without hurting anybody, injuring anybody. But don't say, "I don't love you, I love God more than you." Sages do not say that. They see God in everyone. Then they love everyone as God. So for them there is no problem.

Turiya is far beyond mind. The word, 'beyond,' means not within the reach of the mind. That which is far beyond mind is within you. So Turiya cannot be a state of mind, because it is beyond the mind. Now, sleep is also not a state of mind because one who dwells in that state which we call sleep is called

Ishwara (God), Purusha, the individual soul or Atman. Deep sleep is the dwelling place of the individual soul. Resting there, he experiences all the states. The states of mind are different from the states of consciousness. The experiencer, is in Prajna, deep sleep. That experiencer experiences all the states of consciousness. States of mind are related to the thinking process and emotions. States of consciousness are fields called the waking state, the dream state, the deep sleep state, and Turiya. In samadhi you are very close to Turiya. In Turiya, the perfect state of consciousness, the mind is completely dissolved in the Self. Of course, in the beginning, you have to use your mind to make it one-pointed so that it does not dissipate and distract you from the work that you are doing. But later on, the involvement of mind is not there. It's beyond the state of mind. As long as you are within the field and state of mind, you are not in samadhi. When you are in samadhi you have gone beyond the domain of your mind. When you have attained Turiya, then you have achieved mastery. You can easily observe everything when you attain the summit. From there you can see above, below, here, there, and everywhere.

ॐ

Chapter 8

Science of Mantra

Mantra 8

सोऽयमात्माऽध्यक्षरमोङ्कारो
अधिमात्रं पादा मात्रा मात्राश्च पादा
अकार उकारो मकार इति ॥ ८ ॥

So'yam-atma'dhyaksharam-omkaro'dhimatram
pada matra matras-cha pada akara ukaro makara iti.

So'yam-atma'dhyaksharam- omkaro
The same Atman, in the realm of sound, is the syllable Aum.

omkaro'dhimatram pada matra matras-cha pada
The states (of consciousness) are the letters and the letters are the states.

akara ukaro makara iti.
The three states (of waking, dream and deep sleep) correspond, respectively, to the letters A, U and M.

Figure 1

Your mantra has a form; all sounds have a form. The sound of Om creates a form (Figure 1). It has not been created by an artist according to his imagination. The sound of Om has produced this image and this becomes its symbol. So this is a symbol of a sound called Om. And that sound represents three states, and the fourth state, Turiya, is called amatra, the soundless state, that is hidden.

When you remember your mantra, you are creating an image in your mind. You have stored many, many images in your mind. There are many grooves in your mind. The many memories in your life have created many grooves in your mind. And your mind is in the habit of flowing in the grooves that you have created. Now, if you want your mind to flow in new grooves that you would like to create, you find yourself helpless. Many a time, students think nothing happens when they are remembering their mantra, nothing happens when they pray. Your mantra is a compact prayer. Instead of saying, "O

Lord give me this and O Lord give me that," one uses the word, 'namaha,' commonly used to complete most mantras. Namaha means, not mine. Nothing belongs to me, everything belongs to Thee. This is the meaning. When you use the word namaha with that feeling, it becomes part of your life and your behavior changes according to that feeling and according to that thought.

So mantra is not only a mere word that creates a form but is a great thought which has a deep impact on your life. It is a great feeling which leaves a deep impression in your life. Now you say, "I have been remembering my mantra and nothing is happening to me, I don't see anything." This is a common complaint. This complaint is voiced by those who do not understand the science of mantra. Is it ever possible to do some action and not reap the fruits of your action? No, it's not. When you are performing an action, you are bound to reap the fruits of your action. When you are remembering your mantra and nothing is happening to you, what does that mean? It means that your mantra is being stored in the unconscious mind and when the time comes, when there is need, the mantra will help you.

When does the need for the mantra arise? Remember one thing. Among all the diseases of the world, there is one most serious disease. We have tried our best to eliminate that disease, but it is still there and is increasing all the time and all human beings have to face it. And that disease is called loneliness. We are all lonely. So when we get lonely we try to enter into a partnership called marriage. Loneliness doesn't go away; then we try to have children. Loneliness doesn't go away; then we try to have pets. Even that does not give us freedom from loneliness. Loneliness still remains. There is only one thing that will give you freedom from loneliness, and that is your own constant friend within, called your mantra.

But have you established friendship with your mantra? I have. Do you have any other friend in the world who is dearer to you than the friend within you? If it is given second position, it won't work. When your mantra, the friend within you, becomes your best friend, then it functions, it will help you always and everywhere. When you are disappointed with external relationships, with the external world, with your ideas, thoughts, desires, then your mantra gives you solace from within and becomes your guide. So when you remember your mantra to such an extent that it becomes your best friend, then your mantra starts talking to you and guiding you. There are many times when I cannot talk to my students, because they will not understand me. They always think that their teacher is an expert, he is perfect. God has also given me a nose, but you don't want me to smell with it because I am your teacher. And if I like a particular smell, you think I am a bad teacher. So there is a gap between your thinking and my thinking. You do things with some ideas; I do things with different ideas. You think I am doing the same thing that you are doing with the same idea, but that's not possible. I am building a house for my community, and you are building a house for yourself. There's a vast difference.

When you talk of behavioral science, it is in-correct, because it's not a complete science, even though it is accepted as a part of science. It's not true that you can be known through your behavior. I can prove it right now. A fool laughs three times upon hearing a joke. First he laughs because everyone is laughing. Second time, he laughs thinking I have not understood the joke, yet I laugh, what a fool I am.

Third time he laughs, thinking, "O my Lord it's too late for me to laugh, I have understood the joke very late." Laughter is the same all three times, but they have different origins. How can you understand behavior from this laughter? So once you establish friendship with you mantra, you will not be affected by the external world. The external world affects you, when you forget your Self. You are constantly identifying yourself with the objects of the world, whose nature is changing, subject to decay, death and decomposition.

Now you are a friend to somebody who is very weak, namely, your body. Your greatest friend is your body. But the body is very weak and shows its symptoms of decay; you feel sad because your friend is decaying. But the moment you come to know, that your mantra is your real friend, you will not be troubled by the decay of the body. Mantra means that which leads you, that which gives you freedom from the agonies and pains of your mind, because it's your mind that stands between you and the reality. It's the mind which creates a barrier for you. Once you understand that barrier, then you try to go beyond that barrier and only mantra can help you. It's the easiest way to cross the barrier of the mind.

I clap my hands and produce a sound. What is the meaning of this sound? Can we find out the meaning of this sound? Yes, if we apply a scientific method for arresting the sound pattern, it will definitely create an image. This whole world is a big image and is full of images. The mantra is constantly creating impressions in your heart and mind. When does it help? It helps when no one else can help you. Mantra is a compact prayer. It could be one syllable, a word, many words, a long string of words, it depends. A time comes at the end of bodily life that is called time of transition. Your beloved wife wants to communicate with you but you cannot hear her because everything is fuzzy. You cannot move your tongue. You want to say something to her, you cannot. You want to express something to your dear child, you cannot; you want to say good bye to you dear friends, to the country, nation and humanity, and you cannot. You are in a period of transition. For ordinary people, it's a day of sadness. But for yogis, that separation is considered a wedding day. They celebrate that day because a wedding is being performed by Nature. In the courtyard of the un-known, the wedding is performed and that wedding is celebrated, because you have worked hard for it your whole life. The conscious mind fails, it doesn't function because you are not in the waking state. You start dreaming, you start going through imagery, but you cannot explain anything, no one helps you. Then you start going towards the darkness of deep sleep. Who is there to help you? You don't have a body, you don't have senses, who is going to help you? So when there is no one to help you, then your mantra, which has been stored in your unconscious mind, comes forward to help you. Don't worry, if this finger is not working, here is the hand that will help. But that happens only if you have befriended your mantra, kept company with your mantra throughout your life. Only then that reservoir becomes active and comes forward. Then your mantra becomes the leader. That's why it is called mantra setu (bridge), Pranava setu, bridge from this shore to the other shore. Therefore, wherever you go, whatever you do, con-stantly remember your mantra.

The greatest day of your life dawns when you achieve conviction in the teachings that you have received, by contemplating these teachings, by studying the books and sayings of the great sages, the great enlightened ones of the past, in all cultures. If the Lord is everywhere then he is in me. The first step of that great day of your life is taken when you start believing that the Lord is in you. That is only logical. Logic says that if the Lord, the Power of powers, Ultimate Truth is everywhere, then where am I? It may be easier to accept that I am in the Lord, because I am a small being, and the Lord is everywhere. And where is the Lord? The Lord is in me also. That completes the logical reasoning.

First step, the Lord is in me and I am in the Lord. Later on you realize that it is not possible for you to separate yourself from the Lord. Not possible! Only one thing should exist, the Lord exists or I exist, you have to decide. But this does not depend on your decision. That truth, Ultimate Truth exists and is everywhere. There is something wrong with your vision, there is something wrong with your eyes, there is something wrong with your concept, somewhere you do not understand that you are separating yourself from the Lord. What is it? It is called ignorance. What is that ignorance? If you think of only one dimension of life, external world, the waking state, then it is ignorance. You, the experiencer, go to another dimension, the dream state, you go to yet another, the deep sleep state, but finally you have to attain the fourth state, Turiya. That you can attain in this lifetime, today, if you are prepared. You have spread yourself to do something different in the external world, and now suddenly you want to attain Turiya. No, first prepare yourself for attaining that which is your birthright; it is a state of consciousness, you can do it.

One of the simplest methods is to remember the Lord's name, not the Lord, but His name. How could you give a name to someone who is nameless? A child who does not know how to speak, what does she say? Mama mama. For her, that word means mother. We do not know anything about the Almighty Lord, any word we use for him is His name. But let us feel His presence by remembering that name within us. A chapel or shrine is where you remember the Lord. When you constantly remember the Lord's name, then you become a shrine, because the Lord lives in you. Then you say that if the human being is a shrine, how can the human being die? A human being doesn't really die. If my garment is worn and torn, I am not dead. If a book cover is torn, the book is not dead. If a pillow cover is torn, the pillow is not dead, only a part changes, the essential part never changes. God does not require you to remember his name; God never says you should remember my name, this is a human necessity. This is a support, this is a way, and that way will finally lead you to that royal house which is called the house of the Lord within you. You cannot be lost. You can get lost in a journey of the external world. This inner journey is a journey without movement where you can never get lost. You don't move, yet you are going ahead, the only journey of its type.

One of the great sages, Guru Nanak said something which and all the bibles of the world also say. *Nanaka dukhiya sab sansara*. The whole world is plunged in sorrow, drowned in the sea of sorrow. Who's happy? *Sukhiya soijo nam adhara*. Happy is he who is totally dependent, reliant, on the name of the Lord. Not on the Lord, he never said Lord, because no one knows what the Lord is. Your mantra is a name of the Lord, sooner or later your mantra will lead you to the Lord. You are happy because you are remembering your mantra. This Om is a bridge. Your mantra is a bridge. Your mantra is a support. Your mantra is that which helps you to come out of this mire of delusion created by the whirlpool of your own thoughts, wants and desires. It is not necessary that it should be a Sanskrit mantra, no. It is not necessary that it should be a Hindu mantra or a Christian mantra, no. Any prayer that you pick up, a compact prayer, short prayer, can be a mantra. *Tasya vachaka Pranava,* the Yoga Sutras say. Om is the designator, the sign post, pointing to Brahman. The representative of that Lord, who is not known, who is not seen, who is beyond, is Om, that is, your mantra. And if you are honestly relying on your mantra, it will sooner or later lead you to the highest. First you have to remember that mantra silently, without opening your mouth.

Kabira, one of the great sages and poets said, *"Mala pher tho jug gaya, gaya naman ka pher, karka, manka chandke, manka manka pher."* "Your whole life you have spent counting the repetitions of your mantra with your mala; counting because you are worldly, you want to count things. You are counting even God's name. Stop it," he says. This is only a first step, only for beginners. How can you move ahead, how can you improve, if your whole life you are standing at the same place?

So that's why Nanak Dev said, *"Sukhiya soijo nam adhara."* Happy is he who remembers the Lord's name all the time without any conditions. Don't put conditions to the Lord. I'm remembering my mantra all the time but I am not getting many dollars. Well, dollars are there in the bank, why don't you go to the bank? Why don't you earn? Why are you using something great for something very gross, very petty? That's the mistake you are committing. Whenever there is something you can't handle, immediately you say, "Lord help me." It's good, but you cannot escape from punishment for your bad deeds. If during that time, mantra tells you, "Sorry, you have done something wrong, I cannot help you." You say, "You are not my friend." You lose faith. That's not good. So mantra remembered to satisfy your egotistical whims is not very healthy. Never apply your mantra, your friend, for anything bad. Keep your friend in reserve, for that day when no one else can help you, where no friend of the world can reach. Why are you giving that friend a simple worldly task which you can do with your own hands, which you can do with your feet, which you can do using other resources, why are you doing this? The best part of yourself is your mantra. Never misuse your mantra!

Do not give your worldly duties to your mantra. Many times you test your mantra. Yesterday I got ten dollars, if I get twenty dollars today, then my mantra is very good. My friend has fever, let me remember my mantra to see if it heals or not. This is not good. You are misusing the mantra. Let your mantra become a guide. Let your mantra become an observer. Do not involve your mantra in such petty things. Oh I am remembering God, but I am still unhappy. This unhappiness is not God's creation. God has created the universe in which the air, light, water, are all free. Free, everything is free, equally free. You think the breath is different for Ford and Rockefeller than it is for you and me? It's free from nature. But when we build a home, we build a world of our own, there comes discrimination. This is my home, this is your home, this is a good home, that is a bad home, this is comfortable, that is not comfortable.

Tell me one thing. The best part of your body you don't expose. The best part of your wealth you don't reveal, you don't tell people how many million dollars you have, you quietly keep it in the bank. The best part of your life is your mantra. Why do you want to create a mockery of it? So please understand this; once you do that you are free. You'll find that somebody is guiding you. Many a time it will happen.

Now if you remember your mantra loudly, it doesn't work well. Mantra is like atomic power, the more you explore the shakti, the power, in the atom, the atomic energy, you will find the shakti is even subtler than the atom itself. You will find more powerful things coming out of what you call no-thingness. Nothingness means where your mind cannot go. Your mind cannot reach there, that's why you call it nothingness. The Bible says that this whole universe has come out of nothing. How is it possible? All scientific laws, all logic, will be finished if you say that this world has come out of nothing. You see that every effect has a cause within it and every cause produces an effect from it. This world has come out of perfection; this world seen with the true eye is perfect. If you deduct perfect from perfect, yet it remains perfect. If you add perfect to perfect, it remains perfect. If you multiply perfect by perfect, it always remains perfect; therefore it is perfect. But for whom? For one who is constantly aware of this truth. Therefore, remember your mantra subtly, in any language you like. You should be comfortable with the language; you should know the meaning of the mantra.

Now the question comes, if your mantra is a sound, is there a meaning to the sound? A sound is known by its vibrations. A harsh sound will give you bad vibrations which you cannot bear. Sometimes children scratch a surface to produce a harsh screech-ing sound and the parents want to run away from there. You tell them to stop, but the children are not affected by that sound, they are insensitive to it. Some sounds are very soothing, for example, when somebody is singing or playing the piano. You like to hear such sounds. Some of the words of the music you can never forget, they haunt you the whole day, they keep ringing in your mind. The best way to remember your mantra is by closing your lips, sealing your teeth. What should be the position of your tongue? The tongue always has the habit of wanting to translate your thoughts, to give them form. So do not let the tongue touch the palate, but let it touch the roof of the mouth. You'll find your japa has improved, it has become easy. Try it. But as long as you are making sounds with your mantra, you are simply counting.

Instead of rushing to the external world with the help of the senses, let your mind go within. So what should you do? Remember your mantra subtly. Now there is competition here. Our whole life is full of competition, is it not? A part of the mind says, I will remember my mantra so subtly that the other part of my mind does not hear it. The other part of my mind says I am so alert, so one-pointed, no matter how minutely, how subtly you remember, I will hear it. You will have to create this kind of competition in your mind. With the help of one part, your mind becomes very subtle, remembers. If the other part is not alert, you'll forget. The other part should not be producing a huge heap of dollars, a bank balance, a girlfriend, or a boyfriend. Simultaneously, both parts of mind should function together, to help each other.

I used to tell my master "What good is this mantra? The whole day I remember my mantra, nothing happens, I am still hungry in the evening. I still cry; I still feel pain." He used to laugh. He said, "Your mantra has not yet become your guide. When you allow your mantra to guide you, it will guide you all the time. Ok, I bless you that your mantra will become your guide." A human being may learn to trust others, but if a human being has not learned to trust himself, there will be chaos in his life. No one trusts himself. He will say, "Swamiji, is it Ok? Mom, is it Ok? Husband, is it Ok? Girlfriend, is it Ok? Wife, is it ok?" Always asking others, wanting confirmation from outside. When you learn to trust yourself, you'll find a great guide within. One is your mantra, another is your natural conscience. And when they meet and work together, they create a great power.

I had a Fiat car, when Fiat cars were first man-ufactured in India. It was a small car. I was strongly, repeatedly, told not to drive that day. My conscience as well as my guru chakra were telling me again and again, "Don't drive today." I was so trained that if I received the message, "Don't go," I would not go, or else I will be punished. I was very obstinate with my master. I said, "Let me see what happens if I go." Why did I do this? Because I had faith that my master would always protect me, no matter what I did. And he did protect me from disaster, but he also said that there is an end to this, never do this again.

But I did. I used to swim in front of the Rishikesh ashram where, at that time, there was no barrage. Every day, I would float and go up to Haridwar, which is 12 miles away. One day, somebody told my master, "He's a great swimmer." He said, "I want to train him to be a great yogi and he's a great swim-mer?!" So he called me and said, "I heard that you swim." I said, "Yes, I love to." He said, "You love to do many things. But I want you to do this thing. All your little loves don't matter, but this love should be so strong that it should not be distracted by your little loves. You love to paint, you love to sing, you like people, you love to do this, and you love to do that. Stop all this. Stick to your main love. Don't swim too much." I said, "Ganges is my mother, she will never drown me." He said, "I am warning you, yet you are not listening to me?!" I said, "No. I will swim." He replied, "Ok, then you've had it."

At Haridwar, in front of Hari-ke-pauri, they have the arti, light ritual, every evening. When I came to that spot, I found a huge whirlpool there, bigger than my eyes could see. I had never experienced that before. I felt as though somebody was holding my neck and pushing me down, and I touched the bottom, with my hands. And again, from there, I was thrown out. When I was thrown out, I took a small breath, but again, I was pushed inside as though somebody was forcibly pushing me. I saw the water whirling all around me. Then I remembered my master. I said, "I promise never to disobey you again, please help me, I have not yet realized." A third time I was pulled in, but when my hands touched the sand, I was able to start swimming and I came out. I have not swum since then.

In swimming I found another very strange thing that Nature creates. Those who are swimmers will understand this. In most rivers and lakes, sometimes you are swimming, and suddenly, you find the whole expanse of water has become very still and you cannot swim. You cannot swim and you are bound to drown. I saw that even great swimmers can drown in such situations. It is not that they do not have skill, they have skill, but sometimes the water becomes so still that they cannot swim. I was warned, I started studying, and I stopped swimming.

When you do anything in excess, you will die in that same situation; it may be a sport, dance, music or writing. A writer who writes all the time will finally die while writing. A singer who sings all the time will finally die while singing. Swami Rama will die while in samadhi. We all have to die; we all have to leave, so it is better to make sure that you will drop this body while remembering the Lord's name. But you cannot remember the Lord's name suddenly, just like that. You can do this only if you have practiced, if you are accustomed to do it, if you have made it a part of your life. You don't have to postpone your duties for this. Go on remembering your mantra all the time, even in the midst of your duties. Make it a point that whatever you do, wherever you go, you will be remembering the Lord's name, even in the bathroom.

There is no set time for remembering the Lord's name, for it's a way, simplest way, known to all the great traditions of the world. The highest level of japa is when japa goes on by itself all the time. That is called ajapa japa. Japa goes on without conscious effort. You get up in the morning and japa is already going on. It means japa has embedded itself in the unconscious mind which is rather difficult. Anywhere you are, japa is going on inside, you are laughing to yourself, japa is going on; you are angry with your children, japa is going on and you are not really angry. This way japa transforms your inner situation, your life. It's something great. All traditions have somehow or other discovered this power of japa. First step is muttering, then it is remembering, then that remembering leads you to consciousness, awareness; that awareness leads you to absolute silence, and then you are remembering japa without any remembrance, ajapa japa, it has become a part of your life. Then there is only the momentum. Have you seen a potter make pots? When he has finished making the last pot, the wheel still rotates; it still has momentum. When you have finished your work, at the last moment of your life, that momentum of the japa, will give you great joy.

A householder, nay, every human being, discovers that in the world there is little joy. Then he tries to search, wants to go to higher worlds, sun, moon, and stars. So no matter where you go in the external world, there is no transformation. Transformation can take place only within you. There is no stain which cannot be cleaned with the help of mantra remembrance. There is nothing which cannot be eliminated from your life by mantra remembrance. There is no fear which cannot be overcome by mantra remembrance. But you have to be persistent, regular; then, subtly, it can lead you to samadhi.

How long will you remember the mantra? Two days, ten days, twenty days? You say I'm on vacation for 3 days, I don't want to remember my mantra. No, that's injuring yourself. If you do not meditate one day, you have gone backwards by one year. Stop inhaling for one day, can you do that? Don't eat your food for one day, don't go to the bathroom for one day, and don't think for one day. When you are doing all this, when nature is functioning in you, why are you not remembering your mantra? The formula is: *Satu deergha kale nairantarya satkara sevito dhruddha bhumi.* O student, learn to sit every day at the same time. You will see that as long as you keep your mind busy with the mantra, then the devil doesn't come near you.

St. Theresa said this very beautifully. Sometimes you study, but you don't dive deep enough into it. Somebody asked St. Theresa, do you believe in evil, in the devil? She said, "I don't have time! As I pray all the time, I don't have time to think of devil or evil." It means that evil and devil are only thoughts, not actuality, not reality. If you are remembering your mantra, you are free from many things: being jealous of others, thinking badly of someone, getting angry with someone, being negative. Nothing will affect you if you are remembering your mantra. When you are attending to something, attend with full attention, but remembering the mantra. When you are silent, remember your mantra with all your love. When you do something again and again and again, you are creating love for that which you are doing repeatedly, because of habit. You actually do not love anybody but you love your habit. Therefore, you persist. Nowhere is there peace, nowhere is there happiness. It is within and that is created by you. The highest of all states, that which is beyond speech, that which cannot be explained, is inexplicable, that great eternal joy, you can attain in this lifetime, when you gently train yourself in the method of going within to your innermost self. And your mantra is the guide.

It's difficult to talk to somebody who is outside you. It's very easy to talk to somebody who is within you. Learn to understand how to have an inner dialogue between you and the Lord. "O Lord of life, I am not content with my knowledge, with the world around me." So the Lord of life, from inside, answers you, "Then go to the subtler world within you. Withdraw your senses from the external world, remember my name." It can be any name, but don't change the name again and again, don't change your posture, don't change your time, have a fixed time, remember this. In the beginning, if your mind and heart do not accept, do it as a duty. After some time, you'll form a habit, and soon you will love that habit. We are all nothing but a catalogue of habit patterns. Your remembering the Lord's name, any name you choose, constantly, in an orderly way, will lead you to one-pointedness of mind and that creates will-power. With that dynamic will you can be successful in the world and at the same time you can be happy within. Happiness and misery are both creations of the human mind. God has manifested the world, O man, learn to create happiness for yourself. It will happen when you learn to go beyond your senses, beyond your mind, and you stay there in Turiya. And that is possible.

Scientifically, by practicing the method I am giving you, you can study your mind. One whose mind is completely distracted is not fit for meditation. One who can concentrate for some time but whose mind is dissipated at other times is certainly better.

Sometimes focusing your mind with the help of japa, remembering your mantra, helps a lot. But that remembrance could be injurious, if you try to synchronize the mantra with the breath. There is nothing wrong with your mantra. Mantra means a word, a syllable, a set of words which will help your mind, will liberate your mind, if you learn to use it. Don't misuse your mantra. There is a technique for applying the mantra. There are only two or three mantras which are used with the breath like Om, So-ham and Ram. They don't break or distort the breath. If you try to remember any other mantra, with your breath, there will be a jerk in the breath. It will not be smooth, but if you remember Om, there will be no jerk. Now, you can use an encephalograph and you can use breath measurements and you will notice the difference. I'm talking about scientific experimentation, the graphs we have made. Mantras like Om, So-ham and Ram can be expanded to be synchronized with the breath. When you are doing japa of most other short mantras, you should do it mentally, but don't synchronize your breath with the japa. It could be physically injurious. Let us understand the anatomy of this fully. With a short mantra, you are doing your japa rapidly, tatatatatatatata. You think by doing japa fast you are doing something great. No, you are injuring yourself because it will result in rapid breathing. Rats and dogs breathe rapidly and have short life spans. If your breath is jerky it might disturb the motion of your lungs and the right vagus nerve; it will not allow the proper coordination between your brain and the heart. That's why this scripture says nothing but Om. That's why before you do japa, before you do meditation, make your breathing calm and serene. Don't just sit down and immediately start remembering your mantra. First make your breathing smooth and serene. If you are rapidly breathing you have not calmed down. Calmness has something to do with your breath; if your breath is not serene how can you calm down? Not possible! That is why before you meditate, you should learn to breathe in a way that makes you calm. Why do you say grace before you eat your food? It is to calm down and stimulate the flow of the digestive juices.

As long you are consciously remembering your mantra, you will not go to yoga nidra. A time comes when mantra is remembered, but very subtly. Of course that remembrance is so subtle, subtler than the breath. Now, when you are remembering the mantra subtly, a time comes when mantra becomes the leader. Your mind is not a leader. If your mind is the leader, then it will throw the mantra aside and give you a different direction. Mantra becomes the leader; accept your mantra as a leader during that time. Let the mind follow the mantra. A state comes when mantra leads you to perfect silence, and mind has to follow it there. When mind is in perfect silence, there comes calmness, joy and happiness. And if you persist, there is no word there, there is no sound there; you attain a state which is called soundless sound and that is a part of Turiya, that is the beginning of

Turiya, that can lead you to samadhi. This is one of the easiest ways.

ॐ

Chapter 9

A, U , M and Beyond

Mantra 9

जागरितस्थानो वैश्वानरोऽकारः
प्रथमा मात्राऽऽप्तेरादिमत्त्वाद्वाऽऽप्नोति
ह वै सर्वान्कामानादिश्च
भवति य एवं वेद ॥ ९ ॥

Jagarita-sthano vaishvanaro'karah prathama matra'-apter-adhimattvad-vapnoti ha vai sarvan kaman-adish-cha bhavati ya evam veda

Jagarita-sthano vaishvanaro'karah prathama matra'
The consciousness experienced during the waking state, Vaishvanara, is A, the first letter of Om.

apter-adhimattvad-vapnoti
A pervades all other sounds and is the first (letter of the alphabet).

ha vai sarvan kaman-adish-cha bhavati ya evam veda

One who is aware of this reality, fulfills all his desires and is successful.

The first letter, A, is of the same nature as the waking state (Vaisvanara). A is the all-pervading simple vowel; all sounds are pervaded by A. The first letter of Om is also compared with the world of names and forms because one is aware of the external world through the conscious waking state. Without the first syllable A, you cannot utter the word Om; similarly, without knowing the waking state, you cannot know the other states of consciousness.

When the knowledge of the external world is revealed through contemplation and meditation, you become capable of attaining the objects you desire and become apta-kama, he whose desires are all fulfilled. Through deep contemplation and meditation, a student becomes aware of the unity of the life force, prana, permeating the entire universe. The aspirant, instead of perceiving different names and forms, experiences the life force alone, which is one of the aspects of the manifestation of consciousness.

To be successful in the world of objects, knowledge of the external world is important, and if this knowledge is acquired, then you are inspired to seek the next level of knowledge. The external world is the world of means, and he who knows how to utilize the conscious mind and apply it to acquire some worldly object is successful. The world of phenomena should be understood and dealt with. Though you may know that the waking state does not give comprehensive knowledge of the other dimensions of life, it is important to understand, utilize, and direct the conscious part of the mind that functions during the waking state. Without this, you cannot successfully maintain relationships, nor have the means for attaining worldly goals.

Let me tell you something. There are two approaches regarding the objects of the world. One approach is to make all the objects of the world means for attaining the highest state of consciousness. When the aspirant adjusts himself to the external environment of the transitory world, then he knows the way of utilizing and approaching all the means of the world as part of sadhana for attaining his goal, which is Turiya. He can use all the means without establishing ownership, without getting attached to the objects of the world. Without cultivating this attitude, it is not possible for him to be nonattached and to have control over the senses. The external world is the world of pleasure and pain—the pair of opposites. The aspirant wants to attain a state of freedom from the pairs of opposites and so examines the external world, but does not find fulfilment. Therefore, he intensifies his search toward other dimensions of consciousness.

The other approach is to understand the external world and make use of it in a way that does not create barriers for you. It is important to know how to live skillfully so that the charms, temptations and attractions of the world do not create obstacles on the path to enlightenment. The aspirant knows that everything in the external world is subject to change, death and decay. He practices his sadhana by understanding the apparent reality and does not become attached to the world of names and forms or waste his time and energy in acquiring more worldly objects than bare necessities.

Those who know how to direct their energy for success in the external world, know how to direct the conscious mind, and make the best use of the waking state. From the data I have collected from various sources, it is clear that ordinary people are not as satisfied and happy as they appear to be. Though they have more than they need, yet they are afraid of the unknown; they do not know how to go beyond the mire of delusion created by the pairs of opposites. But those who have realized this, search for perennial happiness by exploring other states of consciousness. He who knows how to make use of the waking state skillfully can have success in the external world, but this success does not lead to enlightenment.

Once in a while, in human life, we receive a glimpse of the apparent reality of this universe and its transitory nature. If such opportunities are utilized by practicing nonattachment during those moments, we will surely attain our goal. This awakening comes in every human mind. There is nothing in the world that can fulfill the desire for everlasting peace, bliss, and happiness The moments of awakening make us aware of the truth, but for lack of practice, constant awareness towards truth remains absent. Thus, human beings suffer on account of their self-created miseries.

In this verse, the waking state is explained as being compared with the world of names and forms, which is related to the first letter of Om, A. But to know the comprehensive meaning of Om, one should learn other aspects of consciousness represented by U and M, and finally to the hidden state of Om, the state of silence, the supreme state of Turiya.

Mantra 10

स्वप्नस्थानस्तैजस
उकारो द्वितीया मात्रोत्कर्षादुभयत्वाद्वोत्कर्षति ह
वै ज्ञानसन्ततिं समानश्च भवति
नास्याब्रह्मवित् कुले भवति य एवं वेद ॥ १० ॥

*Svapna-sthanas-taijasa   ukaro   dvitiya
matrotkarshad-ubhayatvad-votkarshati ha vai jnana-
santatim samanash-cha bhavati nasyabrahma-vit
kule bhavati ya evam veda.*

Svapna-sthanas-taijasa ukaro dvitiya matro
**The consciousness experienced during the
dreaming state is U, the second letter of Om.**

matrotkarshad-ubhayatvad-votkarshati
**The dream state is an elevated state between
the waking and sleeping states just as U is an
elevated intermediate sound between A and M.**

*ha vai jnana-santatim samanash-cha bhavati
nasyabrahma-vit kule bhavati ya evam veda.*
**One who knows this subtler state is superior
to others and in his family, knowers of Brahman
will be born.**

The second letter, U, is of the same nature as the
dreaming reality (Taijasa). When the sadhaka
(aspirant) becomes capable of analyzing and realizing
the nature of U, the dreaming reality, through deep
contemplation and meditation, he attains knowledge
of and mastery over his unconscious mind. The

dreaming state deals with the world in terms of symbols and ideas rather than objects and is thus a subtler state and closer to the Truth. This world of ours is a conception, an idea. It is the idea that is the basis for the worldly structure. Therefore, the idea of the architect is superior to the construction. A sadhaka who realizes the state of U can inspire others, for he unfolds the mystery of ideas and creativity, both. Being the middle letter, U, the intermediate state, is more subtle than and superior to A, the first, as the dream state is an intermediate state and subtler than the waking state.

The experiencer experiences waking, dreaming, and sleeping realities, and during these experiences, finds himself absorbed in a particular state and not aware of the other states. When he analyzes his role in different states as sleeper, dreamer, and experiencer of the external world, he wonders about and wants to understand the entire field of consciousness and witnesses it collectively by attaining a state beyond. During dreams, he is not aware of the external world. In this state, only the past impressions from the unconscious are recalled. Now tell me, can anyone dream according to their wishes? The dream state is beyond the control of the ordinary person's conscious mind. When the experiencer is not in touch with the objects of the world through the senses, the flow of those suppressions and repressions comes forward from the unconscious. Though it interrupts the mind while moving towards the sleeping state, yet it offers an opportunity for the sadhaka to analyze his desires, motivations, feelings, and thoughts. After analyzing the nature of the mind and its modifications, he becomes aware of the subtle impressions, or samskaras, that create the objects of dreams. He then overcomes negative mental attitudes such as animosity, jealousy, and hatred.

Dream is the product of unfulfilled desires. The mind flows in the grooves of its unfulfilled desires and creates a predominant habit pattern. Thus dreams are worth analyzing to help us understand the predominant habits of our minds. In dreams, the aspirant discovers the dark corners of the unconscious mind where lurk hidden desires. It is like lifting the carpet in a room, and finding the hidden layers of dust and dirt. But a burning desire for attaining the sumum bonum of life can annihilate all other desires, feelings, and thoughts. Then, the sadhaka goes beyond this turmoil and experiences that higher dimension for which he was longing.

That which cannot be dealt with by the mind during the waking state is dealt with during the dreaming state. That is why it is called a more subtle state than the waking state. This state is therapeutic because in it we have an opportunity to express ourselves the way we want to. All the unfulfilled desires, thoughts, and feelings which for some reason are not fulfilled during the waking state, come forward to create a dreaming reality. We cannot dream of something we have never seen, imagined, heard of, or read about. During the dreaming state, we are rewarded and whipped at a more subtle mental level. It is a finer state than the waking state. We can magnify all of our desires and fears in dreams because dreaming is a self-created state.

There is a vast difference between the dreaming state and that of meditation and contemplation. During the dreaming state, there is no control, and we are not conscious and in control like we are in the waking state. In meditation and contemplation, we consciously place ourselves in a concentrated and undisturbed state. During meditation, we remain fully awake and conscious, in full control. During dreaming, we are not conscious, and the unconscious impressions appear whether we want them to or not. In the dreaming state, we have no control, but in meditation, we have perfect control. In meditation, the mind is trained to maintain one-pointed focus voluntarily. This gives the meditator an opportunity to judge, analyze, and decide the usefulness of those impressions coming from the unconscious that can create dreaming reality. During meditation, the meditator can experience all that is experienced during the dreaming state. He is fully conscious though he is not utilizing his senses and not contacting external objects. When the conscious state is expanded, dream analysis becomes clear, and the ideas and symbols that are experienced during that state are easily understood. If we have clear introspection, the harmful and injurious dreams that strain and distract the mind and drain its energy can be analyzed and resolved. All conflicts that are at the root of dreams can also be resolved. A time comes when meditation stirs the unconscious mind, and brings forward impressions from its hidden corners. That aspect of mind that dreams and the energy that is consumed by dreaming can be brought into creative use and channeled for higher purposes. It quickens the method of analyzing, understanding, and surveying the whole dreaming state.

Actually, this Upanishad makes the aspirant aware that dreams alone are not the subject for analysis, but that the entire dreaming reality should be understood thoroughly.

The dreaming state is represented by the letter U, which comes between A and M. For knowing Om in a comprehensive way, we have to move to higher dimensions of consciousness. The higher dimension here, means the sleep state. This state is represented by the letter M, the last letter of Om. After examining all the joys and pleasures of the external world, finally we yearn to have a deeper quality of joy during sleep. Consciousness withdraws itself from the waking state and the dreaming state and goes to the restful state of deep sleep.

Mantra 11

सुषुप्तस्थानः प्राज्ञो मकारस्तृतीया मात्रा
मितेरपीतेर्वा मिनोति ह वा
इदं सर्वमपीतिश्च भवति
य एवं वेद ॥ ११ ॥

Sushupta-sthanah prajno makaras tritiya matra miter-apiter va minoti ha va idam sarvam-apitish-cha bhavati ya evam veda.

Sushupta-sthanah prajno makaras tritiya matra
The consciousness experienced during the deep state of sleep is M, the third letter of Om.

miter-apiter va minoti
The letter M, is the measure, and that into which other sounds dissolve.

ha va idam sarvam-apitish-cha bhavati ya evam veda.
One who knows this state is able to comprehend all within himself.

The third letter M is the deep sleep state (Prajna). By constantly remembering Om, A and U become one sound and dissolve into M. The pronunciation becomes OOOOMMMM: thus, A and U are dissolved into M and again are evolved from M. In this way, Prajna, M, is the source that contains and measures A and U, which emerge from and merge into it. He who realizes that the letter M is identical to Prajna, becomes capable of realizing the nature of the internal and external worlds. He is also able to realize his oneness with the entire universe.

The sleeping state indicates that consciousness has the power to withdraw and expand itself. He who knows that it functions both externally and internally is definitely superior to one who has explored only the waking and dreaming states.

During ordinary sleep, the mind remains withdrawn from the dreaming and waking states. This restful period is essential for healthy living. But it is not necessary to waste eight to twelve hours for sleep and yet wake up tired. Such a supposed need is a mere myth, a tradition without truth. The human body, even after exhaustion and fatigue, does not need more than three hours of sleep, provided the art of sleeping is understood and practiced correctly. Wasting time and energy leads to the habit of inertia and sloth, which is not helpful even for ordinary people. Actually, the quality of sleep is more important than the number of hours slept.

A real meditator does not sleep the way ordinary people sleep; sleep is brought under his voluntary control and will. He determines to sleep and then to wake up whenever he wants. This is the art of yoga nidra, which is practiced by meditators. The sleeping state is more subtle than the waking and dreaming states, and he who knows how to utilize this state of yoga nidra can benefit himself immensely. He can give rest to his body, nervous system, brain, and mind, and he can expand his consciousness and know that which is unknown to ordinary minds.

During deep sleep, there is the experience of the void; the same void can be experienced during meditation. That void is not empty, but there is a feeling of emptiness. During that time, there is no content, and that is why it is called deep sleep. So sleep is an unconscious state without content; there is no awareness. When one is in the void, he does not know that he is in the void, but once awake, he remembers being in the void. In deep meditation, he is in the void and aware of it at the same time. The meditative state is a fully awakened, expanded state. By following the law of expansion, the sadhaka goes on expanding his consciousness to the extent of Universal Consciousness, and then one loves all, and remains in perennial joy all the time. The experiences of this dimension are very subtle. Fortunate is he who has already explored the waking, dreaming, and sleeping realities. He is a highly evolved aspirant who prepares himself for the last part of the journey, namely Turiya.

Mantra 12

अमात्रश्चतुर्थोऽव्यवहार्यः प्रपञ्चोपशमः
शिवोऽद्वैत एवमोंकार आत्मैव
संविशत्यात्मनाऽऽत्मानं
य एवं वेद य एवं वेद ॥ १२ ॥

Amatras-chaturtho' awyavaharyah prapanch-opashamah shivo' dvaita evam-omkara atmaiva samvishaty-atmanatmanam ya evam veda.

Amatras-chaturtho
The soundless aspect of Om, is Turiya, the fourth state.

avaharyah prapanchopashamah
This aspect of consciousness is not com-prehended by the ordinary mind and senses and is the state of cessation of all phenomena.

shivo' dvaita evam-omkara atmaiva samvishaty-atmanatmanam ya evam veda.
This is a blissful state, one without a second (advaita). Om is the real Self. One who knows this expands himself to Universal Consciousness.

The soundless aspect of Om, silence, is of the same nature as the fourth state, Turiya. Turiya has no parts and is incomprehensible, being beyond speech and mind. It is the state in which all doubts and conflicts are resolved. It is the final state of Om, into which A-U-M have merged. It is the state of merger of the waking, dream and deep sleep states. It is the non-dual and blissful state that is the cessation of the grand illusion called Maya. It is identical with Atman, the very Self of all individuals. He who knows this state of Absolute Reality expands into the Supreme Self, realizes himself and is not born again.

The waking, dreaming, and deep sleep states are states where duality is experienced, for the ex-periencer is different from the experience. But the fourth state, Turiya, is a nondualistic state which is compared to the silence into which one is lead by Om. All sounds actually arise from silence, so this state can be termed as soundless sound. That is why it has been given the name Turiya. If one stands on the banks of a river, he hears the sound of the river as it flows. When he goes back to the source of the river, he discovers that there, there is no sound. The sound grows as one moves away from the source. The meditator is going to the origin of the sounds, which is perfect silence, the state beyond, called Turiya. In deep meditation and contemplation, a state is attained in which truth is realized, the real Self is realized. Such a state is inexplicable, for the weight of this truth is so heavy that the mind and speech cannot hold it. Therefore, no words can explain this perennial joy. From the summit of this realization, the sadhaka can comprehend the knowledge of all states of consciousness simultaneously and collectively, and thereby attain the state of enlightenment.

Appendix A

Prana, the Link between Body and Mind

Prana means life and life means prana in the external world. Our everyday experience is that we cannot live without that prana. We receive prana through food, we receive prana through our breath, we even receive prana through our pores. There are many agencies through which we receive prana. Now this prana is always in touch with its source, the original prana. I am talking of Adi-prana, the first unit of life. It is through the agency of Adi-prana that Atman or Brahman manifests all the animate and inanimate objects of the world. With the help of that first unit of life, this entire universe comes into existence. Mind, the consciousness manifested in living beings, animate beings, is the agent of the supreme prana. But even inanimate objects are projected, manifested, by the original prana which is also called Maya.

I am not talking of the breath which becomes the vehicle for prana, supplying energy for internal states. Thus, breath is a projection of mind. The breath you inhale is called prana, but actually breath is not prana, remember this. Breath is breath. It is called vayu, air, in Sanskrit. We find air everywhere. Is it breath? No. Because, there should be something living, something conscious, to direct it. This vayu is like ashwa, a horse. A horse cannot go to its destination unless there is a rider. There is a rider on this breath we are inhaling called prana; otherwise it's only vayu. Vayu is the horse and prana the rider who directs it. So prana is something living; it's not mere dead air, it's not just a mixture of oxygen, nitrogen and other gases. No, there is a conscious entity called prana that is riding on vayu and leading it.

Now let us try to understand more about this prana that we inhale. You can live without food for many days, but you cannot live without breathing for even a few minutes. A yogi can, through practice, become aparna, one who lives only on air. He can live for a long time by taking prana from the air, without taking any solid foods. As this is not possible for ordinary human beings, I am not going to discuss it any further.

We get prana through food, but the prana that is supplied by food is not enough, is not complete. So we receive prana through breath. Breath is a vehicle to supply prana. There are vehicles within, mainly two vehicles, inhalation and exhalation, called prana and apana. Now they are doing their duties. The mind is definitely superior to these two vehicles. Sometimes mind may get disgusted and say, "You are a bad person, don't do this; till now you have been righteous, but now you have taken the wrong path." If you are nasty to your children, spank and scold them or if you don't behave nicely with your wife, your mind will tell you and this is true. But prana will never deny you, never reject you, no matter who you are or what you do. If you are a criminal, prana will never deny you. You may be the worst person in the world; even God may not have a suitable punishment for you because you have gone beyond the mire of punishment, yet prana will not abandon you. Why? Prana is our mother. No matter what happens, a real mother will never abandon her child, infant child. She will protect her at any cost, without any discrimination. For her, a child is a child. Mind is like a father. What does a father do? If a son wants some money from his father, the father will ask, "How many rupees do you want, how many dollars do you want?" Five, ten, twenty, one hundred, there is always some limit. But mother never says I will give you only so much milk, and no more. Take as much as you want, no conditions. So as an infant, you have an unconditional relationship with your mother. I am talking of a normal mother, not a crazy mother or an extraordinary mother.

So prana is like our mother. Mind is like our father who discriminates. Mother and father live together, they have a close relationship. Breath and mind are called twin laws of life. To understand the mind, you will have to understand your breath. To understand your breath, you will have to understand your mind.

Now, suppose I say Om, and concentrate here, where the upper lip meets the nostrils. The breath will be very fine. Breath will not be shallow, but will be very subtle. Shallow breathing is not good for you, but a yogi's interpretation is that the breath has become fine because he has withdrawn consciously and started breathing subtly. Sant Jnaneshwar, one of the greatest yogis born in Maharashtra just a few hundred years ago, says, "You are the string of breath and you can easily go from this prana to the other prana, adi prana." The first unit of life, is called prana and this breath is also called prana. That which helps in manifesting this world is prana, that which helps in manifesting jivas, souls, is called Brahman. There is a difference. Prana manifested the world but not human souls. I am talking of manifestation, not creation. From one, two, three, four, five, many, can be manifested; this is manifestation of the One becoming many. Suppose you are sitting in a dome of many colors. All the colors have been manifested from only one color, white; this is called manifestation of one. So Brahman is responsible for the manifestation of individual souls, just as the ocean is responsible for the manifestation of waves. So there is a difference between Brahman, the One who manifests the jivas or the individual souls, and Maya which manifests the universe of objects. Prana and Maya are one and the same. Adi-prana is the origin of the prana we are exhaling and inhaling.

What is the relation between this prana we are inhaling and exhaling and that original prana that manifested the universe? There is a relationship. Let me draw a line. You, the individual self, are at one end of the Reality, and the other end is called Absolute Truth. If the two ends of the line are brought together into a circle, then you are one with the Absolute, you can never be separated from the Reality. Have you observed that in many traditions, rings are exchanged as a symbol of marriage, of bride and groom coming together as one? So also, jiva and Brahman are made one, united, and that is called yoga, that unification is called yoga. So what is this marriage? Yoga, union, is the marriage, where individual soul is made aware of the Reality, made aware that the ultimate goal is to become one with the Reality that is within, not far away.

Pure concentration is when one thought continues for a long time, without intervening thoughts. How can one thought flow continuously? If something is very pleasing to the mind, then the mind likes to flow in that pleasant groove. Mind means energy, and this energy flows through the many grooves of habit patterns. What can you do? You can consciously make new grooves, so that the mind stops flowing through the old grooves and flows through the new channels that you have created. It is a new training program for the mind, a method of transformation.

Now let us study, in depth, something about breath. You may not have beaten me physically, but if you give me some bad news which affects my mind, I will start crying and you will see tears flowing from my eyes. I may have a nervous fit, I may even faint and become unconscious. The bad news may even affect my heart and cause heart failure. How does it happen? During that time, what happens to our breath? If you study this whole process, you'll understand how wonderful and unique it is. It will be very useful for you to understand something about your breath. Many people are very particular about their diet and that is good. But no matter how wonderful your diet is, you will not be healthy if you do not learn how to breathe. Pranas play their own important part. When you receive the bad news, the breath is not serene. No, it becomes very shallow. Shallowness of breath is very close to death. Shallow breath is related to an imbalanced mind. Whenever you are imbalanced, whenever you are agitated within, whenever you are emotional, whenever you are irresponsible, you will find that your breath has become shallow, not fine, but shallow. Fine breath is made consciously; shallow breath is made by your bad habits. Then you do not fill up to the depth of your lungs and breath becomes very shallow. And during that time, mind does not know what to do, mind becomes weak, because you are not supplying the proper energy; the right volume of blood is not going from the pumping station called the heart to the brain. You will find the same condition if somebody hits you or gives you a karate chop. There will be a loss of blood supply to the brain. And during that time, the brain does not function well. You may be very powerful and strong, but if hit by a person who has the right training in the martial arts, the right balance, you will become uncoordinated and look in the wrong direction and will not be able to use your physical strength properly.

The mind can make your breath shallow. The mind is a catalogue of habit patterns. Habit patterns are created in the mind because of our repeated actions, repeated speech, repeated thoughts, repeated foods, repetitions in our daily life. So when I hear some bad news, that impulse directly affects my mind and my mind immediately, from within, starts crying, and tears start flowing from my eyes. The mind can destroy the body, can make the body unhealthy or miserable. Why? The whole of the body is in the mind, but the whole of the mind is not in the body, this is the underlying principle. The whole of the body can be understood better through the mind. This is a way of understanding the body through mind, not mind through body.

If you don't allow your breath to become shallow, whenever such a situation arises, you will not cry, you will not sob, you will not become sad, you will not be grief-stricken. For being sad and sorrowful, your breath has to be shallow. That's why it is said, "Don't have shallow breath." Learn not to have shallow breath, not to have jerky breath, not to create a long pause between inhalation and exhalation. This pause is a key point, because pause is death. Suppose I inhale and never exhale, I am dead; if I exhale and never inhale, I am dead. All the yogic kriyas, all these practices and exercises are done to control that pause. If you are able to control the pause between inhalation and exhalation, you are a great yogi. An advanced yogi is one who knows how to control the pause between inhalation and exhalation. Pause means death. Death is constantly hovering at the gate of life, but you can keep death away; you can stop her knocking at the door of your life if you do not allow that pause to be increased or expanded unconsciously, this is my point.

What is the best way to regulate your breath? Sometimes you can measure your breath, but this will happen only when you have knowledge of the tattwas or elements. Your body is a compound of five elements, namely, earth, water, fire, air and space. Sometimes the earth element is predominant, sometimes the water element, and so on. The predominant element will definitely affect your breath. Take a piece of mirror and exhale on to it and observe the pattern formed on the surface by the vapor in your exhaled breath. It might, for example, create a moon shape for you, but if you repeat the experiment after an hour or two, you will find that the shape has changed, because a different tattwa is predominant now. In the mountains, we do not have sophisticated machines for experiments, but we know the right experiments! You'll find that the vapor coming out of your mouth makes many shapes because of the influence of tattwas. One day you may find your body is aching all over; this is the influence of vayu tattwa, the air element. Another day, you'll feel very hot; this is the influence of the fire tattwa. If you are feeling very hot, don't say your kundalini (dormant energy at the base of the spine) has been awakened. We never encourage such delusions in the student. If a student says his kundalini has been awakened, he should be able to read a book with his eyes blindfolded. If he can read blindfolded, yes, it is awakened; if he cannot, it is not. All these symptoms can mislead you. Sometimes you like to think that you know, although you do not know. There's a part of you that wants to feel that you are better than others, even if that's not true. That part of you should not be encouraged.

Now, how to regulate the breath? Whenever any shocking thing happens, become conscious of your breath and keep it from becoming shallow. One day, we were at Dr. Ballentine's home. There was a rake there and Mahima, Kevin Hoffman's wife, stepped on it and fell down. She fell down and lay there like she was dead. So I told Kevin to go and check on her. He said, "No, it's O.k." I said, "Why don't you go?" He said, "She's relaxing." I protested, "She's hurt and you say she is relaxing." He said, "I know her." So I asked her, "What did you do?" She said, "I was hurt, so I composed myself, I was breathing well."

Now, this teaching was also passed on to their children. Once, Kevin's son, a small child, by chance inserted his finger between a door and the frame and a nail pierced right through his finger, from one side to the other. It was a shocking sight. Everybody came running; somebody cut the nail but it took some time for that nail to come out. But he was not shaken, he remained composed and strong. That was the result of the parents' inner strength. How can you make your children strong? You have to be strong, if you want your children to be strong, this is my point. Strength comes from within, and that strength comes from balance. The more you learn how to have balance in your life, the stronger you will become.

Only a yogi can know which element is predominant by internally observing his breath. But at least you can watch your mind and breath. If your breath is calm, definitely you are helping your mind and it becomes easy to calm your mind. What is the most balanced period in your life, when you can establish balance in your mind, in your breath and in your body? For that the five tatwas have to be in balance. You should not allow any one tattwa, any one element, to become predominant. How can you do that? It is not easy to manipulate your tatwas, but you can work with the breath. Breath is the barometer of both your mind and body. It's a bridge between the two shores of body and mind; and it's not something dead; it's something living because there is someone directing it. The day that someone withdraws that prana, there will be air but there will not be life; life is not mere breath. Life is prana and prana is life.

When you sit down to meditate, you should first compose yourself, make yourself calm. Just saying, "calm down" is not enough; that calmness does not last for a long time. Is there any other way? Yes. It is called sushumna awakening. If you are attentive, you will gain a lot and in just one day, the first time you practice this, you will have a glimpse of what I am saying. If I say 2 and 2 make 5, you might, out of reverence, keep quiet but that's foolish. But what I am going to tell you is based on experiment, based on experience.

Before meditation, you have to learn to make your pranas, the pranic sheath, serene. Look at this point where the upper lip meets the nostrils. That should be the point of focus to compose yourself and make the breath serene. If you are able to do that, then you will be able to awaken your sushumna. In a scientific way, sushumna awakening is very important. Sushumna awakening means you have three channels of energy. Normally there are only two active channels, one channel of energy flows though your left nostril (ida), another channel of energy flows through your right nostril (pingala). Experiments have been conducted in many universities showing that flow through the right nostril will give warmer air and that through the left nostril, cooler air, because the electrical potentials of the two nostrils are different, their nature is entirely different. Suppose this nostril of mine is closed. I can open it up by concentrating on it. It will start flowing. Any nostril that is blocked can be made active by concentration on it. It means concentration on any part of the body can activate that part of the body. Many of you complain that you think of sex all the time. If you think of sex all the time, even during meditation, you can become a sex-maniac because you are concentrating on nothing but sex. So concentration activates. Through concentration, even a paralyzed part can be cured. This is how biofeedback works. Biofeedback is based on concentration. Suppose something happens to this part. If I concentrate on this part, there will be good blood flow. Concentration can cure blocked arteries. Blocked arteries can be created by your bad breathing, shallow breathing. Coronary heart diseases have something to do with shallow breathing. Westerners do not have patience to train for a long time to reach perfect poise. They prefer short cuts. I am leading you through a short cut. But the shortest cut of all is to just cut your ego, nothing higher than that. To do this is very difficult.

Yoga teachers ask you to concentrate on the ajna chakra, eyebrow center, with breathing exercises, to increase your memory and intellect. For this is the gateway to the city of life. The teacher will give you concentration at the vishuddha chakra, throat center, if you are an artist, dancer, musician, or writer. If you are very emotional, the teacher will give you concentration at the anahata chakra, heart center.

This chakra has two intersecting triangles, one upward and the other downward. The upward triangle indicates ascending power, that is, human effort. The downward triangle denotes descending power or grace. Where grace and human effort meet, that is called the Star of David, or anahata chakra. Those who are emotional can concentrate here, and with the help of that emotional power, they attain the higher state of ecstasy. Those who are not healthy will be advised to concentrate on the manipura chakra, navel center. Why? Because, close to the manipura chakra is the beginning of the biggest network of energy channels in the body, called khanda, a solar system, not just a fireplace. The teacher will not allow you to meditate on swadhisthana chakra, because otherwise, the whole day you will be thinking of sex. With sexual diseases like frigidity and impotency, concentration on this chakra may be given.

Practicum 1: Diaphragmatic Breathing

Although breathing is one of our most vital functions, it is little understood and often done improperly. Most people breathe in a shallow and haphazard manner, going against the natural rhythmic movement of the body's respiratory system. Diaphragmatic breathing, on the other hand, promotes a natural, even movement of breath that strengthens the nervous system and relaxes the body.

The principal muscle of diaphragmatic breathing, the diaphragm, is a strong, dome-shaped muscle. It divides the thoracic cavity, which contains the heart and lungs, from the abdominal cavity, which contains the organs of digestion, reproduction, and excretion.

The diaphragm is located approximately two finger-widths below the nipples in its relaxed or dome-shaped state. It comes up slightly higher on the right side (between the fourth and fifth ribs) than it does on the left side (between the fifth and sixth ribs). In the center the diaphragm is located at the xiphoid process, the lower part of the sternum. The rectus abdominus, the two strong vertical muscles of the abdomen, work in cooperation with the diaphragm during diaphragmatic breathing.

During inhalation the diaphragm contracts and flattens; it pushes downward, causing the upper abdominal muscles to relax and extend slightly and the lower "floating" ribs to flare slightly outward. In this position the lungs expand, creating a partial vacuum, which draws air into the chest cavity. During exhalation the diaphragm relaxes and returns to its dome-shaped position. During this upward movement the upper abdominal muscles contract, and carbon dioxide is forced out of the lungs.

Diaphragmatic breathing has three important effects on the body:

1. In diaphragmatic breathing, unlike shallow breathing, the lungs fill completely, providing the body with sufficient oxygen.

2. Diaphragmatic breathing forces the waste product of the respiratory process, carbon dioxide, from the lungs. With shallow breathing, some carbon dioxide may remain trapped in the lungs, causing fatigue and nervousness.

3. The up and down motion of the diaphragm gently massages the abdominal organs; this increases circulation to these organs and thus aids in their functioning.

In diaphragmatic breathing a minimum amount of effort is used to receive a maximum amount of air; thus, it is the most efficient method of breathing.

Technique

Lie on the back with the feet a comfortable distance apart. Gently close the eyes and place one hand at the base of the rib cage and the other on the chest.

Inhale and exhale through the nostrils slowly, smoothly, and evenly, with no noise, jerks, or pauses in the breath. While inhaling, be aware of the upper abdominal muscles expanding and the lower ribs flaring out slightly. There should be little or no movement of the chest.

Practice this method of deep breathing three to five minutes daily, until you clearly understand the movement of the diaphragm and the upper abdominal muscles. The body is designed to breathe diaphragmatically as is clearly seen in a newborn infant. This should again become natural and spontaneous.

Practicum 2: Sushumna Application

For meditation you have to establish tranquility. And for that, the method is sushumna application, a simple method of breath awareness. To begin the process of sushumna awakening, ask your mind to focus on the space between the two nostrils, where the nose meets the space above the upper lip. Focus the mind on the breath as it flows past this point. This first step in learning sushumna application is learning to change the flow of your breath with your mental ability. To accomplish this process you must learn to create a relaxed focus on the right or left nostril. If the nostril is blocked, then when the mind focuses on it, that nostril will become active. When you have learned to mentally change the flow of the breath in the nostrils, then a time comes when both nostrils begin to flow evenly. This may take some months or even a year, depending on your capacity and the burning desire within you. When both nostrils flow freely, that is called sandhya, the wedding of the sun and moon, or ida and pingala. Once this experience can be maintained for five minutes, the student has crossed a great barrier, and the mind has attained some one-pointedness and becomes inwardly focused. When the nostrils flow evenly, the mind cannot worry because it is disconnected from the senses. Then, the mind attains a state of joy that is conducive to deep meditation.

Practicum 3: Two to One Breathing

This is called an emergency breathing exercise. You can do it anywhere, on a plane too. You have to be still while doing it, that's all; you cannot do it while walking. You have to be either sitting or lying down. Don't do it while standing, you might fall. So lie down in shavasana. Always use a pillow, thin pillow, otherwise, sometimes urdva vayu or apana vayu, the gastric gases, may create a disturbance. Upward movement of the apana, used up gas, should not disturb you. O.k.? Lie down in shavasana. Gently close your eyes and physically relax your limbs, all limbs, systematically upwards from toes to your head and again come down, just physically relaxing. Start breathing diaphragmatically; this is very helpful. Then, as I told you, let your mind follow the breath. The easiest way of concentrating the mind is to let the mind flow with the breath. Mind is very close to breath, but mind is not sincere to the breath. Through breath, you should learn to approach your mind, for mind and breath are twin laws of life. For a few minutes do diaphragmatic breathing, this is very helpful. That should become a habit.

The diaphragm is the strongest muscle in your body. With the help of it, you can even lift a grand piano. Its flexibility is lost if we do not use diaphragmatic breathing. As you exhale, push in your abdomen; then let it come out gently as you inhale. Don't exert yourself when you are releasing your abdominal muscle, only use your effort when you are exhaling, pushing in. If you are not doing this, you are not inhaling enough, according to your capacity, as much you should. You can eliminate any condition of your mind, any sorrow, any sadness, by this type of breathing. Whenever you are sad, just breathe deeply and you are free. Whenever you are going through any emotional problem just breathe deeply and you are free. You are accumulating toxins inside, and those toxins are injurious to your whole being, that's why you are miserable. You should not allow those toxins to build up in your body. You build up these toxins through food, through breath, and through thinking.

Try to relax your limbs and muscles as much as you can. First you have to exhale, that's called rechaka. Let your mind flow with your breath, because they are the greatest friends in the world. If breath is calm, it can help to make your mind calm. When you go beyond your capacity in exhalation, there will be a jerk. You have to watch your capacity. First you should use a ratio of 8 to 4, exhalation to a count of 8 and inhalation to a count of 4. I am just giving you the starting ratio. Later, it can be increased. Any respiratory problem or any emotional problem can be nipped by this method; it's very therapeutic for the mind and for the breath. It's very good for the heart, nervous system, and brain. Your memory will improve if you follow this method. The ratio of 8 to 4, 8 counts exhalation and 4 counts inhalation, is used in cloth mills, mines and other polluted places, where you find particles getting into your lungs. When you are afraid that your lungs are being polluted by such particles, practice this type of breathing 2-3 times a day, 5 minutes at a time. When you inhale it goes to your storehouse, the lungs, and when you exhale you are forcing toxins like carbon dioxide from your lungs and all the muscles in which toxins are distributed. You are forcing your whole system, lungs and all muscles, to release carbon dioxide and you are inhaling to your full capacity. This is very healthy.

Appendix B

Yoga Nidra

Yoga nidra is a simple method consisting of a few breathing and mental exercises. To practice it, lie down on your back in the corpse posture (shavasana) in a quiet and undisturbed place, using a pillow and covering yourself with a blanket. The surface should be hard, and the pillow should be soft. Start doing diaphragmatic breathing. After twenty inhalations and exhalations, as you inhale, visualize an incoming wave of the ocean and as you exhale visualize the wave going back into the ocean. After ten or fifteen breaths, the shavayatra, 61 point exercise, should be carefully done.

Then learn to divest yourself of thoughts, feelings, and desires, but see that you do not touch the brink of sleep. The space between the two breasts, which is called anahata chakra, is the center where the mind rests during this practice. The mind should be focused on inhalation and exhalation only. While exhaling, the mind and breath are coordinated in a perfect manner. The mind observes that the inhalation and exhalation are functioning harmoniously. When the breath does not go through the stress of jerks and shallowness, and there is no unconscious expansion of the pause between inhalation and exhalation, then it establishes harmony. Beginners, for lack of practice, are trapped by inertia, and in most cases they experience going to the brink of sleep. This should be avoided in all cases. One should not pursue the practice at this state, but should just get up and then repeat the same process the next day. This practice of emptying yourself and focusing on the breath should not be continued for more than ten minutes in the beginning, and it should not be practiced more than once a day, for the mind has a habit of repeating its experience, both unconsciously and consciously. In habit formation, regularity, punctuality, and a systematic way of practice should be followed literally.

Technique of Shavayatra

Lie in shavasana; relax completely for one to two minutes. Bring your attention to the point between the eyebrows and think of the number "1." Keep the attention fixed on that point for one to two seconds. In the same manner, continue concentrating on the points and corresponding numbers through point 31 (Figure 2).

Repeat the exercise twice. Practice for seven to ten days. When this exercise can be done without allowing the mind to wander, then continue through all 61 points.

Practice the 61 points exercise after relaxation and before pranayama (breathing exercises). The exercise may be begun on either the right or left side, but be consistent. If you begin (on the torso) with the right arm, then in the lower extremities also begin with the right leg. The sixty-one point exercise should not be practiced when you are sleepy or tired.

61 Points Exercise

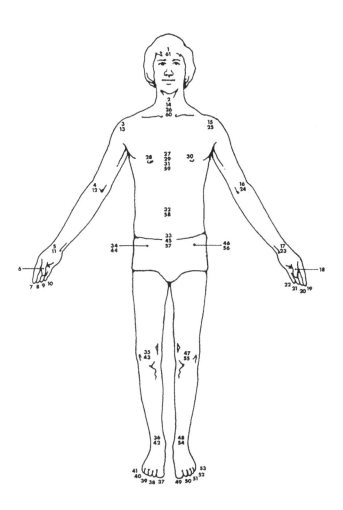

Figure 2

Appendix C

Om Kriya

This kriya, or yogic practice, is a unique method for deepening your concentration and meditation. In this kriya, you can attain a state of deep bliss, like that of sleep, but you remain conscious. It is a state which is beyond sleep, between sleep and Turiya. These exercises are not demonstrated or explained outside the monastery but I am teaching it because many of you have been with me, practicing, for many, many years and I think you should know this kriya. And it will help you. This method you can use for yourself, and you can also use it on others; it is a scientific method. If you do not misuse it you can go ahead. It is very good for those who suffer from insomnia and cannot get a good night's rest. It also helps improve memory. Do this practice when you are not tired, when you are not going to sleep, when your tummy is not a pantry, when you are not very hungry, and when you have not eaten. You can do it at any time but it should not be done for sleep. This is a very good technique, a very therapeutic technique, but it should be done regularly. Habits, engagements, desires, break that which is called persistence. When a doctor says to use a medicine for 10 days, how does he know that in ten days time you will be all right? It means that he has done experiments before with the drug. So is the case with this science. If you persist for some time, I can tell you, after so many days, this is going to happen, after so many days, that is going to happen. But if you do not practice, but just want to know, that is not right knowledge. I hope you practice and help yourselves. Perhaps you'll find a new vision, perhaps you'll find something new.

This kriya is done in a posture which is called shavasana. Shavasana means corpse pose. You lie down on your back in this posture, called shavasana, with your heels spread apart and with your arms away from the body, palms upward and fingers gently curled. Now suppose you are in this pose, and I say, "Hello, how are you?" and you say, "Fine," then you are not like a corpse. Corpse pose means you should entirely pose like a corpse. A corpse does not speak, does not see, hear, or move; if somebody hits the corpse, it does not open its eyes. First, you should learn to acquire that state which is called the corpse pose, though your consciousness will be present. You should be fully conscious, but put your body in that position. One of the highest poses is the corpse pose; in itself, it is perfect.

The word shava, means corpse. What is this word? Why is it called shava? It is missing something, it is missing shakti. Shiva, without shakti, becomes shava. If you don't have energy, you are inert, mere shava, mere corpse. During that time you should not be active at all. Make your body completely inactive but comfortable and conscious. Then you are relaxing. How will you relax? Not with suggestions, no. Suggestions will give poor relaxation, a hypnotic relaxation. If, instead, you exhale and allow your mind to flow with the breath, then all toxins will be expelled because you are lengthening the exhalation. All the carbon dioxide, used up gas, will rush to the lungs, the storehouse, and be expelled.

There are very few people for whom this posture is not suitable; most people like to lie down. There are, however, two obstacles in this posture. First, you might go to sleep and second, you might urinate; it can happen if your bladder has lost its power of conduction. That is why Shankaracharya and other yogis, did not recommend this. But if you decide you are not going to sleep, no matter in which posture you practice, you can deepen your meditation in this posture definitely. It's as definite as 2 plus 2 equals 4, not 5. Whether you are good or bad, whether you are a sage or a criminal, this will definitely deepen your concentration.

The room should not be very warm, nor very cold. The floor should not be very hard, nor should it be very uneven. Don't do this practice on a waterbed! The floor may be hard, but you can put a mattress on it and use a soft pillow. The pillow should be soft and the bed should be hard, remember this. Always use a pillow, thin pillow, otherwise, urdva vayu or apana vayu, the gastric gases, may create a disturbance. Many of you complain of an aching body. If you come to me, first I will ask you what type of bed do you use. What type of pillow do you use? If you twist the pillow and insert it under the neck, in the morning you will feel some pain and the doctors will advise you to wear a collar. Many a time you turn from side to side and use a hard pillow and that disturbs you. Often the bed disturbs you. Make your room less bright, without harsh lights that distract your eyes.

Lie down in shavasana. Gently close your eyes and physically relax your limbs, all limbs, system-atically upwards from toes to your head and again come down, just physically relaxing. Start breathing diaphragmatically; this is very helpful. Then, as I told you, let your mind follow the breath. The easiest and best way of concentrating the mind is to let the mind flow with the breath. The mind is very close to breath, but the mind is not sincere to the breath. A husband may not be faithful to his wife, running here and there. The mind is like that man, while the breath is like a mother, they have different natures. A mother tries to control the father in her own way; so if you approach through your mother you can easily have access to your father. But if you approach your father first, perhaps you will meet with denial. Through breath, you should learn to approach your mind, for mind and breath are twin laws of life. For a few minutes do diaphragmatic breathing, this is very helpful. That should become a habit.

Try to relax your limbs and muscles as much as you can. First you have to exhale, that's called rechaka. Let your mind flow with your breath. No one can attain as good a friendship as mind and breath. If mind wants to distract breath, breath is always distracted; you will not be healthy. If breath is made calm, it can help make your mind calm. Now you are allowing your mind to flow with the breath, exhaling. If you go beyond your capacity in exhalation, there will be a jerk. You have to watch your capacity. So you should work with the digital system. First you should use a ratio of 8 to 4, exhalation to a count of 8 and inhalation to a count of 4. I am just giving you the starting ratio. Later, it can be increased. I am bypassing many breathing exercises, nadi shodhanam or channel purification, other exercises like antar (internal) and bahya (external) kumbhaka (retention), plavni, etc. I am bypassing all that in establishing this kriya.

Figure 3

Om Kriya

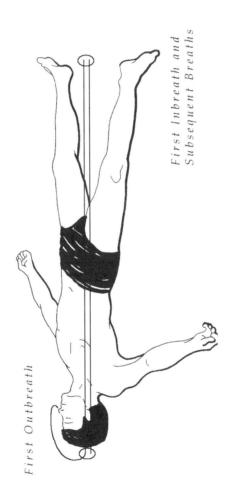

First Inbreath and
Subsequent Breaths

First Outbreath

The first exhalation is from the bridge between the nostrils to the top of the crown and then down, to the space between your heels. Then you are inhaling from the space between the heels to the top of the crown. After that, you are inhaling and exhaling from the top of the crown (see Figure 3). If you have not practiced to lengthen your breath, then exhale only upto the point where both legs unite, called muladhara chakra. There is a triangular cavity at the base of the spinal column where sleeps kundalini shakti, called power of powers, coiled, some say 2-1/2 feet, but definitely 3-1/2 times. It is here in this cavity. Many names are given to it. When she is sleeping here, we are in the waking state. Because she is sleeping here, we are still brutes. Why is she sleeping here? Because she's intoxicated; the power of consciousness is the intoxicant. How does this happen? When you are intoxicated you forget your home, your own home. Her real home is actually at swadhisthana chakra, the pelvic center. But because of intoxication, she forgets and she is sleeping at muladhara. Swadhistana is her own abode. Swa means own, adhistana means abode. Yogis learn to awaken that sleeping serpent energy.

If you can, try to go with the length of the breath that will be very useful to you. Yogis even measure how many inches the breath flows during exhalation, 4 inches, 8 inches, 10 inches. As you are exhaling, let your mind follow. Don't create a pause, start inhaling, going to the crown of your head. Again with no pause, start exhaling from the top of the crown to the space between the two feet again. Only the first exhalation is from the space between the nostrils. After that, you exhale from the top of the crown. Initially, you should do five exhalations and inhalations. Then, gradually increase the number to 100 exhalations and in-halations.

If you have not practiced lengthening exhalation, better exhale down to the muladhara chakra first. After a month or two you can go down to the space between your feet. After 3-4 months you can make a point somewhere in the distance, feel as though you are exhaling to that distance, to that point, and inhaling from there. Do not visualize a wall in front of you; let there be a clear blue sky. You can gradually increase the distance mentally. Now there are two aspects. One is called door darshita, seeing far and wide. You can see something beyond the walls. The other is called sukshma darshita, seeing the subtlest. You can see the subtlest thing. A small pin is dropped here; immediately you can spot it.

Now, slowly as you learn to expand the length of exhalation, go on expanding, don't visualize any wall in front of you, visualize an open window, visu-alize as though you are going towards the horizon, towards space. Where does this stream of exhalation go? You'll find that it flows into a pool, the stream becomes one with the pool. This is a pool of cosmic energy. Now you are going to inhale. Here's something very mysterious. From where are you inhaling? You are not inhaling from the nostrils. From where are you inhaling? You are inhaling from the pool of cosmic energy, filling yourself to the depths of your being. Who is giving you this life breath? We take different foods, we have different thoughts, but we have only one air to inhale. There is only one proprietor who is giving us air to inhale. That means there is only one proprietor of your body. This Upanishad says it's prana, asleep in the city of life. How can you go to the city of life? When you go there you should not fall asleep. If you know the technique of being awake, yet being there, then you will know that Purusha. You can enjoy His presence with yoga nidra; it can be done.

When you exhale, you have a feeling of emptying yourself. In inhalation you reverse that feeling by filling up your whole being which you have emptied. One feeling you use when you exhale, another feeling you use when you inhale. Otherwise, you may remain in that state and lose touch with the life force and remain inactive. With one feeling you empty your whole system, with a different feeling you fill up that system. What mantra can you use? You can use Om, it's very supportive. Mantra is a great support. When do you need support? When you are weak, mantra is a great support. You should have friendship with the mantra, then it helps you whenever you need support. You are remembering the mantra Om, a single syllable. Your feeling will be entirely different when you do this kriya. No matter how much meditation you have done, you will be transported into a different realm when you start doing this kriya.

Now when you are doing this you can use Om, because Om will direct the flow. It's like that fish that does not touch either shore, but only follows the flow. It is like that bird which flies freely in the blue sky. So you are exhaling, not mere exhaling, but with Om. Half of the sound is OOOO and half is mmmm , Om. And then you are in the state of amatra, you have gone to silence. Mind should watch the breath with only one Om during inhalation, another Om during exhalation. As a sound, it's only one sound.

There are three channels in your body. The channel in the center is called centralis canalis and on both sides are two ganglionated cords. Energy is flowing through the central channel, and kundalini is residing at the base. A originates from the top of the crown, U rolls down and by the time you reach the end of exhalation, it becomes M, then silence. Then, you come back the same way to the top of the crown. You visualize the breath flowing through that channel called centralis canalis, the middle channel. You can go beyond the body; let it go, but as long as you are in the body, there is a system.

During exhalation, feel that you are emptying your body. You can easily locate the tension points in your body. Now when inhaling, feel that you are filling up to the depths of your being, the energy received from the atmosphere, from the cosmos. That's a true feeling, that's not something artificial. While exhaling, see how far you can go with your breath stream. After visualizing that distant point, come back filling to the depths of your being, with fresh energy. You should visualize a clear, blue sky. Every time you exhale, you have to advance a little further with the stream of your breath. Let me see how far you can go with the stream of breath when you are exhaling. And your mind should flow with the breath, it should not run here and there leaving that stream of breath. Then pull in the stream of energy from that distant point, filling your whole depth. O.k.? Because you are doing this with breath awareness, it is not self-hypnosis. If you are not doing it with breath awareness, then you are only giving suggestions to yourself. "You should go to sleep, you should go to sleep, you should go to sleep." This is called self-suggestion. Now, for some time let your mind flow with the breath. If anything intervenes, you under-stand what is intervening, something very ugly, bad habit of yours, or something important which you have forgotten to do.

Your breath should not be jerky; it should not be noisy; it should be calm. Let your mind flow with the flow of breath, but during that flow, when you are exhaling, you are exhaling all that you have; you want to throw away everything that you have. If a glass is full, how will you put something in it? You will have to empty it first. Even the empty glass has something in it called air. When you fill it, then it will be filled. That is the process. Some people, no matter how old they are, look very fresh, young, because of this practice. Your skin will change, that's the first symptom. Your skin will become very smooth like silk; your face will become very loving, your eyes will become very piercing. These are certain symptoms that I observe in students.

You might not feel like coming back. Slowly you'll find your body is really floating, it might even float in space, and it's not difficult. That floating experience will give you great joy. Step by step you should practice, that's my point. Don't jump. Learn to be patient with yourself. Always have an alarm clock for this practice so that you will not be afraid, but will come out at the right time. You should use an alarm clock or ask somebody to wake you up at the right time. Now, you have to follow the system.

Choose a time for this kriya when all interruptions are avoided. After 10 days, 15 days, one month you can expand your exhalation beyond the muladhara chakra to the space between your feet. If you do it for 15-20 days, you will feel elevated; you will find your personality has changed; your thinking has changed; and your memory has sharpened. I am not making mere statements, this is a fact. What problems will you find? You'll discover all the bad things arising from shallow breath, all the diseases connected with shallow breath, diseases coming from jerky breath, diseases coming from noisy breath, diseases coming from pause. It's a very therapeutic practice. If you are a therapist, you can teach your patients this practice, and even monitor their progress without seeing them, from a distance.

You will have many, many, many wonderful experiences. Don't push yourself, go according to your capacity otherwise you will feel as though someone is squeezing you. Increase your capacity gradually. I was instructed and I did this experiment with other students like me. We had a three month course in which we attained what the teacher told us would happen. I always used to tease my teachers in a funny way. If something happened, I would say it didn't happen. I wanted to know whether the teacher was sure or not. He said, "You are lying." I said, "No." He said, "Then you are not fit for this place." Only then I agreed, "You are right. I only wanted confirmation." From the very beginning, I had that bad habit; they were kind enough to tolerate and accept this foolishness of mine; but now I reap the same fruits, my students do the same thing to me!

Earlier I told you only about going further and further with exhalation. You have to complete the kriya by reversing this. Slowly you will have to learn to come back, come back gradually with the same 2:1 ratio. Voluntarily you reverse the expansion and bring it back to this point between the two nostrils. During that time, your inhalation and exhalation are very fine and you are exhaling and inhaling between the eyebrow center and the bridge between the nostrils. The brain has a reserve of prana for about 3 minutes, after which the brain starts degenerating. As you can live for 2-3 days without eating food because of body reserves, so also with prana there is a reserve for about 3 minutes. After 2-1/2 to 3 minutes the brain starts degenerating and that's called death. You are conscious, but you float in great joy, you might even levitate, provided you have done it perfectly. It may take 3-6 months to attain this, but joy you will attain the very first day you start practicing.

So when you are exhaling and allowing your mind to flow, the whole body is getting relaxed. I once demonstrated that when the body is completely relaxed, you cannot lift that body easily. It will take 6 or 7 people to lift the same body which can normally be lifted by two people. Heaviness is a symptom of how relaxed the body is. But it's only at the level of body consciousness. You should feel delight in relaxation, but you should not get afraid. In the beginning, do not practice more than 5 minutes. Do you know that 10 minutes practice with one-pointed mind will lead you to samadhi? Some of you say that you meditate for two hours. I say no. You sit for two hours of course, but you do not meditate for two hours. Your effort is to make your mind flow towards its target, without any interruption. You can do it with the help of this kriya.

There are 4 main states of consciousness, waking, dream, deep sleep and Turiya. Then there are three intermediate or transitional states, unmani, ahladini and samadhi, making a total of seven states. (See Figure 4). Between waking and dream, is the intermediate state called unmani. Between dreaming and sleeping is the intermediate state called ahladini. Between sleep and Turiya is the intermediate state called samadhi. If you perfect this kriya, then it will become easy for you to do yoga nidra. Yoga nidra is very close to samadhi. Yoga nidra is also called sleepless sleep or voluntary sleep. In sleepless sleep you are in deep samadhi, yet you are fully conscious. Many of you think that in deep samadhi you are not aware. No, no, no, your awareness expands. Don't lose your awareness in any situation. When your

Figure 4

Four States of Consciousness

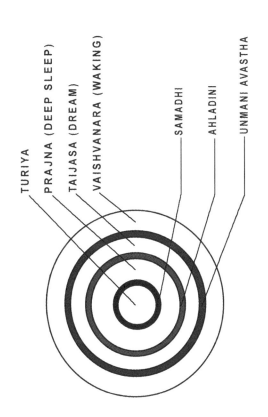

awareness slips to the valley of absent-mindedness, that's not a good sign. It should be intact.

There is a Sanskrit book that is called *Duti-vigyanam. Duti* means messenger, and here it has been used for pulse. *Vigyanam* means knowledge. With the help of the pulse one can diagnose disease. Allopathic doctors don't have this skill and wonder how it is possible. They have not developed that skill. It can be done without seeing a patient, without knowing where the patient is, by telephone, even without telephone if there is a true connection. But, this is possible only when the mind starts flowing freely without any interruptions. For a few days interruptions will come. When these interruptions start decreasing, you'll find the mind is flowing freely with the breath, breath is flowing freely with the mind, and there is great joy. During that time, sushumna is activated. Sushumna means sukha mana, peaceful mind, joyous mind, serene breath and calm mind. That state which is given by serene breath and calm mind is called sushumna, where both nostrils start flowing freely. Neither nostril is predominant, both start flowing freely. And when they both flow freely, you cannot cry, you cannot have pain, you cannot have sadness, because that state of breath leads your mind to a state of joyous mind.

Now, medical science says that you have more than 10 billion brain cells, but these cells are constantly dying, and there is no rejuvenation of the brain cells according to medical science. But a yogi says, of course, they can be rejuvenated. We never say that all the dead cells can come back to life, like the miracle of Christ. We don't say that, but we have a method of not allowing the cells to die. How will it help you? If out of 10 billion cells, a few cells die every day, who cares? Well, in old age you lose your memory, you lose your physical coordination, you may even become insane. The brain is the seat of the mind which is energy; the brain is a physical part. If you constantly blast my seat, I will be disturbed all the time. Don't constantly blast your brain. You are blasting your brain because you are not breathing well. You are blasting your brain through bad food. You are blasting your brain with negative feedback: you are good for nothing, you are bad, you are this, you are that; as you talk to your husband you are talking to yourself. If you are saying something to somebody, it means you are talking to yourself, you are saying the same thing to yourself. It's a projection of your mind. So don't do that, stop blasting.

How? Mind will do it, so you have to keep your mind busy all the time so mind doesn't do that. Whenever the mind is idle, give it some work. Don't allow the mind to be free, it can become the workshop of the devil. That is why you have to remember the center of consciousness within. Those who are Jewish, can remember some sort of confirmation which they use, prayer, compact prayer. Those who are Christian can use some saying of Christ. Those who are Hindu can use some mantra. Otherwise you can use the method recommended by the Upanishad that your state is the fourth, Turiya. You are a citizen of the fourth, and the three countries for which you have a visa to travel freely are waking, dreaming and sleeping. But where is your real country? Your real country is Turiya, it is your permanent abode. With this type of thinking, you can slowly reduce wandering from this country to that country and stay in your own native place that is called Turiya, the state beyond waking, dreaming, and sleeping.

About the Author

Swami Rama was born in the Himalayas in 1925. He was initiated by his master into many yogic practices. In addition, Swamiji's master sent him to other yogis and adepts of the Himalayas to gain new perspectives and insights into the ancient teachings. At the young age of twenty-four he was installed as the Shankaracharya of Karvirpitham in South India. Swamiji relinquished this position to pursue intense sadhana in the caves of the Himalayas. Having successfully completed this sadhana, he was directed by his master to go to Japan and to the West in order to illustrate the scientific basis of the ancient yogic practices. At the Menninger Foundation in Topeka, Kansas, Swamiji convincingly demonstrated the capacity of the mind to control so-called involuntary physiological parameters such as heart rate, temperature and brain waves.

Swamiji's work in the United States continued for twenty-three years and in this period he established the Himalayan International Institute of Yoga Science and Philosophy of the USA. Swamiji became well recognized in the US as a yogi, teacher, philosopher, poet, humanist and philanthropist. His models of preventive medicine, holistic health and stress management have permeated the mainstream of western medicine.

In 1989 Swamiji returned to India where he established the Himalayan Institute Hospital Trust in the foothills of the Garhwal Himalayas. Swamiji left this physical plane in November, 1996, but the seeds he has sown continue to sprout, bloom, and bear fruit. His teachings embodied in the words "Love, Serve, Remember" continue to inspire the many students whose good fortune it was to come in contact with such an accomplished, selfless, and loving master.

Himalayan Institute Hospital Trust

The Himalayan Institute Hospital Trust was founded in 1989 by Swami Rama. It continues to grow through his extraordinary grace.

It includes one of the best equipped, modern hospitals in Asia, a medical college with extremely high standards, a nursing school, and mobile clinics and satellite centers to serve the many outlying villages.

Unique are its focus on preventive and curative health care, and on evolving a new pattern of medical education and health care by incorporating the spiritual basis of life in relation to health and modern technology.

Most important, many of the 15 million people in the region who have faced suffering with little or no health care can now look forward to having access to modern healthcare services for themselves and their families.

For information contact:
Himalayan Institute Hospital Trust
Swami Ram Nagar, P.O. Doiwala
Distt. Dehradun-248140, Uttarakhand, India
Phone: 91-135-247-1200, Fax: 91-135-247-1122
e-mail: info@hihtindia.org   www. hihtindia.org

Swami Rama Foundation
of the USA, Inc.

The Swami Rama Foundation of the USA is a registered, nonprofit and tax-exempt organization committed to the vision of the Indian sage, Swami Rama. The Foundation was established to provide financial assistance and technical support to institutions and individuals who are ready to implement this vision in the USA and abroad. The essence of Swami Rama's vision lies in bridging the gap between Western science and Eastern wisdom through the integration of mind, body, and spirit.

For information contact:
Swami Rama Foundation of the USA, Inc.
2410 N. Farwell Avenue
Milwaukee, WI   53211   USA
Phone: 414-273-1621
info@swamiramafoundation.us
www.swamiramafoundation.us

The Essence of Spiritual Life
a companion guide for the seeker
Swami Rama

This concise collection of Swami Rama's teachings serves as a practical guide for the spiritual seeker. Spiritual practice leads the seeker towards inner experiences of divinity that further one towards attaining the goal of life. Swami Rama, yogi, scientist, philosopher and humanitarian, was deeply steeped in the spiritual traditions of the Himalayan sages. He was a free thinker, guided by direct experience and inner wisdom. His teachings are universal and nonsectarian, providing a bridge between the East and the West.

ISBN 978-8-1901-0049-6; $12.95, paperback, 136 pages

SAMADHI
the Higest State of Wisdom
Yoga the Sacred Science, volume one
Swami Rama

Yoga the Sacred Science brings Patanjali's Yoga Sutras to life in a very personal and helpful way.

Swami Rama's description of the totality of the mind, the functions of the mind, and the emotions, goes far beyond the concepts of modern psychology, and provides insight into the intricacies of yoga psychology, making this an invaluable edition from the therapeutic viewpoint as well as its practicality as a guide for living a healthy, balanced life.

ISBN 978-8-1881-5701-3; $14.95, paperback, 256 pages

Available from your local bookseller or: To order send the cost of book plus $2.50 for the first book and $.75 for each additional book (within US) (Wi. res. add 5.5% sales tax) to:
Lotus Press, PO Box 325, Twin Lakes, WI 53181, USA
Toll Free: 800-824-6396
Phone: 1-262-889-8561; Fax: 1-262-889-2461
lotuspress@lotuspress.com;   www.lotuspress.com

Let the Bud of Life Bloom
A Guide to Raising Happy and Healthy Children
Swami Rama

Let the Bud of Life Bloom

A Guide To Raising
Happy And Healthy Children

SWAMI RAMA

"Childhood is pure. If we impart good education to our children, become selfless examples for them, and give them love, perhaps they will grow and become the best citizens of the world. Then, the whole universe will bloom like a flower."

In *Let the Bud of Life Bloom*, Swami Rama gives us relevant, practical insights into forming the basis of a happy life through a happy childhood. Through blending the best of our ancient values with new inventions, children can grow into healthy, creative adults.

ISBN 978-8-1881-5704-4; $12.95, paperback, 100 pages

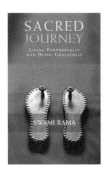

Sacred Journey
Living Purposefully and Dying Gracefully
Swami Rama

To understand death, a person must try to understand the purpose of life and the relationship between life and death. The two are partners, each providing a context for the other.

This book is about the relationship between life and death, and the 'how and why' of organizing one's life in a way that leads to expansion and growth, and that is helpful in preparing for the transition we call death.

ISBN 978-8-1881-5700-6, $12.95, paperback, 136 pages

Available from your local bookseller or: To order send the cost of book plus $2.50 for the first book and $.75 for each additional book (within US) (Wi. res. add 5.5% sales tax) to:
Lotus Press, PO Box 325, Twin Lakes, WI 53181, USA
Toll Free: 800-824-6396
Phone: 1-262-889-8561; Fax: 1-262-889-2461
lotuspress@lotuspress.com; www.lotuspress.com

Conscious Living
A Guidebook for Spiritual Transformation
Swami Rama

This is a practical book for people living in the world. The word "practical" implies that the teaching can be practiced in the world, in the midst of family, career and social obligations. No prior preparation is required for reading this book, and after reading this book, no further teaching is required. If one were to sincerely practice the teachings presented by Sri Swami Rama in this book, one would surely achieve the goal of self-realization, a state described by Swamiji as the summum bonum of life, a state of bliss, a state of perfection.

ISBN 978-8-1881-5703-7; $12.95, paperback, 160 pages

Conscious Living
An Audiobook for Spiritual Transformation
Swami Rama

This 5-CD set is a collection of lectures that Swami Rama gave in Singapore in 1991 and 1992. Recorded live, they capture the essence and inspiration of Swamiji's public speaking style. His book, *Conscious Living: A Guidebook for Spiritual Transformation* is derived from nine of the lectures he presented in Singapore. Five of those lectures are included in this new audiobook.
Volume one: Prayer, Meditation, Contemplation, 56.40 min.
Volume two: Freedom from Stress, 57.45 min.
Volume three: Creative Use of Emotions, 62.01 min.
Volume four: Mind and its Modifications, 45.31 min.
Volume five: The Goal of Life, 43.08 min.
ISBN 978-8-1881-5718-1, 5-CD set, $29.95

Available from your local bookseller or: To order send the cost of book plus $2.50 for the first book and $.75 for each additional book (within US) (Wi. res. add 5.5% sales tax) to:
Lotus Press, PO Box 325, Twin Lakes, WI 53181, USA
Toll Free: 800-824-6396
Phone: 1-262-889-8561; Fax: 1-262-889-2461
lotuspress@lotuspress.com; www.lotuspress.com

Bhole: Adventures of a Young Yogi
inspired by the childhood stories of Swami Rama

by Hema de Munnik

This is the story about a boy named Bhole who was born in a remote village in the Himalayan Mountains of Northern India. Bhole was adopted by a great saint and raised in a cave monastery from the age of three. He loved to play pranks on meditating monks and his unruly behavior often disturbed the peaceful and quiet atmosphere in the cave. After a few years he was sent to school in his village, where he shared adventures with his dog Bhaiya, and with his friend Arjun. During his holidays he met with many yogis, saints and sages who amazed him with their supernatural powers. He wanted to become a yogi, but before this could happen he needed to remove many obstacles and had to overcome many difficulties.

ISBN 978-8-1881-5737-2, $18.95, pb, 352 pages

Available from your local bookseller or: To order send the cost of book plus $2.50 for the first book and $.75 for each additional book (within US) (Wi. res. add 5.5% sales tax) to:
Lotus Press, PO Box 325, Twin Lakes, WI 53181, USA
Toll Free: 800-824-6396
Phone: 1-262-889-8561; Fax: 1-262-889-2461
lotuspress@lotuspress.com; www.lotuspress.com

Bhole Prabhu Sings
Swami Rama

As a young man Swami Rama was known as Bhole Prabhu. He was an accomplished musician who played the veena and loved to sing. But one day his master became concerned about his one-pointed devotion to music. He was worried Swamiji would neglect his meditation practice and made him promise not to sing again until 1985.

The first song on this recording, Guru Vandana, is the piece Swamiji sang as a young man when he was known as Bhole Prabhu, on All India Radio. All of India wept when they heard it. We are pleased to release these very rare early recordings of Bhole Prabhu, as well as the later pieces of Swami Rama in this edition.

ISBN 978-8-1881-5710-5, $14.95, audio CD, 62.08 minutes

AUM
a meditation in sound
Swami Rama

On the banks of the holy river Ganges in northern India, is an ancient Shiva temple where in 1988 Swami Rama recorded this chanting of AUM. As you listen to this simple yet profound recording, you are carried by the singular voice of Swami Rama chanting AUM with only an electronic tanpura for accompaniment. Mysteriously this sound grows and grows throughout the recording though no instruments have been added. Finally the entire temple is vibrating and reverberating with this cosmic sound spiraling throughout the shrine as it stimulates the temple bells to sympathetically resonate.

ISBN 978-8-1881-5708-2 , $14.95, 36.52 minutes, audio CD

Available from your local bookseller or: To order send the cost of book plus $2.50 for the first book and $.75 for each additional book (within US) (Wi. res. add 5.5% sales tax) to:
Lotus Press, PO Box 325, Twin Lakes, WI 53181, USA
Toll Free: 800-824-6396
Phone: 1-262-889-8561; Fax: 1-262-889-2461
lotuspress@lotuspress.com; www.lotuspress.com

The following books by Swami Rama are available in Spanish:

Spanish translaton of *Conscious Living*
Vivir Consciente
Una Guía para la Transformación Espiritual

Spanish translation of *Let the Bud of Life Bloom*
Dejad que el Brote de Vida Florezca
una guia para criar niños sanos y felices

Spanish translation of *Sacred Journey*
Viaje Sagrado
Vivir con Propósito y Morir en Gracia

Spanish translaton of *The Essence of Spiritual Life*
La Esencia de la Vida Espiritual
una guía que acompaña al que busca

Spanish translation of *Samadhi the Highest State of Wisdom*
SAMADHI el Estado Más Elevado de Sabiduría
Yoga la Ciencia Sagrada, volumen uno

Available from your local bookseller or: To order send the cost of book plus $2.50 for the first book and $.75 for each additional book (within US) (Wi. res. add 5.5% sales tax) to:
Lotus Press, PO Box 325, Twin Lakes, WI 53181, USA
Toll Free: 800-824-6396
Phone: 1-262-889-8561; Fax: 1-262-889-2461
lotuspress@lotuspress.com; www.lotuspress.com